THE hello, FEARS CHALLENGE

A 100-DAY JOURNAL FOR SELF-DISCOVERY

Michelle Poler

ILLUSTRATED BY SOPHIA ARAUJO JACOBS

 sourcebooks

Copyright © 2022 by Michelle Poler
Cover and internal design © 2022 by Sourcebooks
Illustrated by Sophia Araujo Jacobs

Sourcebooks and the colophon are registered trademarks of Sourcebooks.

All rights reserved. No part of this book may be reproduced in any form or by any electronic or mechanical means including information storage and retrieval systems—except in the case of brief quotations embodied in critical articles or reviews—without permission in writing from its publisher, Sourcebooks.

This publication is designed to provide accurate and authoritative information in regard to the subject matter covered. It is sold with the understanding that the publisher is not engaged in rendering legal, accounting, or other professional service. If legal advice or other expert assistance is required, the services of a competent professional person should be sought.—From a Declaration of Principles Jointly Adopted by a Committee of the American Bar Association and a Committee of Publishers and Associations

All brand names and product names used in this book are trademarks, registered trademarks, or trade names of their respective holders. Sourcebooks is not associated with any product or vendor in this book.

Published by Sourcebooks
P.O. Box 4410, Naperville, Illinois 60567-4410
(630) 961-3900
sourcebooks.com

Printed and bound in the United States of America.
POD

Dedicated to **NOAH**

May we build together an arch of courage, so you can sail through life's challenges turning obstacles into opportunities. Love, Mom

CONTENTS

INTRODUCTION   **VII**

PART 1. HELLO, LIFE   **1**

Day 1	2	Day 6	16
Day 2	6	Day 7	18
Day 3	10	Day 8	20
Day 4	12	Day 9	22
Day 5	14	Day 10	24

PART 2. HELLO, ~~FEARLESS~~ BRAVE   **27**

Day 11	28	Day 16	42
Day 12	32	Day 17	44
Day 13	34	Day 18	46
Day 14	36	Day 19	48
Day 15	38	Day 20	50

PART 3. HELLO, SOCIETY   **53**

Day 21	54	Day 26	64
Day 22	56	Day 27	66
Day 23	58	Day 28	70
Day 24	60	Day 29	72
Day 25	62	Day 30	74

PART 4. HELLO, YOU — 77

Day 31	78	Day 36	92
Day 32	80	Day 37	94
Day 33	84	Day 38	96
Day 34	88	Day 39	98
Day 35	90	Day 40	100

PART 5. HELLO, HATERS — 103

Day 41	104	Day 46	114
Day 42	106	Day 47	116
Day 43	108	Day 48	118
Day 44	110	Day 49	120
Day 45	112	Day 50	122

PART 6. HELLO, EGO — 125

Day 51	126	Day 56	140
Day 52	128	Day 57	142
Day 53	130	Day 58	144
Day 54	134	Day 59	146
Day 55	138	Day 60	148

PART 7. HELLO, GROWTH — 151

Day 61	152	Day 66	166
Day 62	154	Day 67	168
Day 63	156	Day 68	170
Day 64	160	Day 69	172
Day 65	162	Day 70	174

PART 8. HELL-(N)O, HECK YES! 177

Day 71	178	Day 76	190
Day 72	180	Day 77	192
Day 73	182	Day 78	194
Day 74	186	Day 79	196
Day 75	188	Day 80	198

PART 9. HELLO, SUCCESS 201

Day 81	202	Day 86	214
Day 82	204	Day 87	216
Day 83	206	Day 88	218
Day 84	208	Day 89	220
Day 85	210	Day 90	222

PART 10. HELLO, FUTURE 225

Day 91	226	Day 96	238
Day 92	228	Day 97	240
Day 93	230	Day 98	242
Day 94	234	Day 99	244
Day 95	236	Day 100 (!!!)	246

100 CHALLENGES LATER: YOU DID IT!   **250**
ABOUT THE AUTHOR   **256**

INTRODUCTION

"WHERE WOULD YOU LIKE TO BE ten years from today?" Have you thought about that? A *simple* question—yeah, right. This had to be one of the most daunting questions anyone had ever asked me before in my life.

If you've asked yourself this, you know that when trying to answer, you want to dream big—but not too big! You want to sound ambitious but humble. You start dreaming of a 150-foot yacht, and somewhere down the line, you settle for a freaking kayak! You don't want to disappoint future you with BIG plans that went nowhere and then feel like a big FAILURE, right?

Once upon a time, I was asked this question by my professor, and it turned my life upside down. I had big ambitious goals, and I realized that I was too afraid to achieve them. I was living my life in a place of fear, and I felt stuck. I realized that I was hungry for success but driven by fear.

Luckily, just as we had our ten-year vision in mind, our professor introduced Michael Bierut's #The100DayProject to us—and a path toward realizing my goals became clear.

THE 100-DAY PROJECT

"If you could do ONE thing, repeatedly, for 100 days in a row, what would you do?" she asked.

The 100-day project is all about creating. One hundred days spent investing in and creating something, anything. The original 100-day project was created by Yale graphic design professor Michael Bierut, who assigned the 100-day project as a workshop for his students from 2006–2011. His requirements for the 100-day project were simple: that his students choose a design operation to repeat every day—any type of design, any medium, so long as they repeated it every day for 100 days and that they somehow recorded their progress. For the final day of the project, he would have each student give a fifteen-minute presentation to the class about their full 100-day experience. The final projects ran the full spectrum of creativity and were nothing short of amazing. Eventually, the concept made its way online, shared by artist Elle Luna on Instagram as #The100DayProject. It has since grown and evolved through social media, and thousands participate each year to spread their wings and grow!

After my professor assigned the 100-day project to our class,

I considered a ton of different creative projects (journaling, meditation, photography) before I ultimately went with the biggest project I could think of.

One hundred days of facing my fears.

In the course of twenty-four hours, I went from a lifetime of "No, thanks" to "Okay...I'll try." I went from reacting to life to becoming intentional about life. I went from autopilot mode to living life to the fullest.

My goal was to become a braver person, but not only for myself. I wanted to become a braver wife for Adam, my husband, and a braver mom for my future kids.

And I did! The journey since has been WILD—wonderful, messy, passionate, and busy...and full of fears faced.

My project, "100 Days Without Fear," changed my life, so I wanted to create and share a similar challenge for others like me—for people looking to break free of their personal limitations and achieve their biggest goals.

If you've already read (or are reading!) *Hello, Fears*, then you know more of my story, along with the basics of facing fear to better yourself and to grow. And good news! The 100 challenges I've created for you to explore follow the ten chapters and themes I established in the book, including:

1. Hello, Life: From Autopilot to Living Fully
2. Hello, ~~Fearless~~ Brave: How to Influence People Positively
3. Hello, Society: Checking Your Own Boxes
4. Hello, You: Becoming Your Authentic Self

5. Hello, Haters: Exposing Yourself and Dealing with Criticism
6. Hello, Ego: Unlearning Failure
7. Hello, Growth: Overcoming the WTF Am I Doing? Stage
8. Hell-(N)O, Heck YES! Learning How to Ask for the Things You Want, Need, and Deserve
9. Hello, Success: How Not to Self-Sabotage Your Way to Success
10. Hello, Future: Grow Through Dirt—Rewrite Your Story

With this road map as your guide, I hope each journal prompt and challenge found within can help you push the boundaries of your own fears and your own goals and help you become a braver person. I believe the challenges are best taken one at a time, one day at a time, so that's how I have set them up, but feel free to do them at your own pace! So long as you are moving forward in the challenge, there's no specific timeline or metric you need to accomplish. This journey is all about YOU. YOU deserve to be living your best life, and if all that's stopping you is YOUR FEAR, we can find a solution to that together!

So to start, you have to ask yourself: **What's the BEST that can happen?** And even: **Where do you see yourself in ten years?**

Outline your specific hopes and goals for where you'd like to be in ten years. Refer back to your answers as the BEST that can happen whenever you're feeling stuck.

What's the BEST that can happen?

ONE
hello, LIFE

FROM AUTOPILOT TO LIVING FULLY

In the Hello, Fears book, this chapter is about doing what we love like no one's watching.

DAY 1

In going through my own 100-day journey, I realized that I didn't have one hundred unique fears but rather seven different core fears. Those are:

1. Pain
2. Danger
3. Embarrassment
4. Rejection
5. Loneliness
6. Control (or lack thereof)
7. Disgust

While all of us may shy away from pain and danger, other fears speak to our own comfort zones. For example, my husband, Adam, is more anxious about the fears that scare me the LEAST and far less afraid of those that scare me the MOST! So while fear is universal, it is also extremely personal.

For today's challenge, I want you to look at your personal comfort zones. Which fears are your biggest, those you are most afraid of? Rank them from #1 (biggest fear) to #7. **I challenge you to identify one specific fear from your top category and work to face it TODAY!**

THE HELLO, FEARS CHALLENGE

DAY 2

All fear categories are united by one key element: the unknown. Fear of the unknown is the main reason we fear something we haven't tried before; we don't know for certain what the outcome will be! However, the more we say YES to new experiences, the more we allow other emotions and joys to enter our life. Surprise, freedom, curiosity, vulnerability, excitement, trust, and connection are just a few of the emotions I encountered in facing the unknown!

Your challenge today is to embrace an unknown! Try something you've never done before but you've always dreamed of doing. It could be as simple and silly as singing a song at the local karaoke bar or wearing a top you've always admired but never thought you could pull off. Or it could be something bigger and more vulnerable, like giving someone in your life that talking-to you have rehearsed countless times in your head. Whatever you choose, write out what emotions and experiences you LET IN by embracing the unknown!

_____

_____

_____

_____

DAY 2

DAY 3

It's impossible to live life to the fullest if you are always looking forward to what's next. Or, put another way, if you're always thinking about what to have for dinner while you're eating lunch, you're not enjoying the meal!

For today's challenge, take a look at your day with an eye on how to make pieces of it more authentic. Do you scroll through your phone while watching a movie with your partner? Set the phone down and see how much more you talk, maybe even cuddle, without a device in your hand! Find a spot in your day that needs you to be PRESENT to truly relish the results (such as connecting with your loved ones, ACTUALLY unwinding, or putting real momentum behind your goals). Use the tracker below to target and track your results!

Routine/ Habit	Current Block	Proposed Change	Results

Routine/Habit	Current Block	Proposed Change	Results

DAY 4

Much like living authentically, we have to try to live outside of our comfort zones. The only way to make life slow down in the best way possible is by generating memories that break the mold, fostering unique moments of joy. New, fresh memories are the spice of life, and such memories only come from trying something new and pushing beyond ourselves.

Today I challenge you to change up your routine. What if you tried a new lunch spot? Reached out to a new group of friends? What if you threw a surprise party for a loved one to celebrate an accomplishment or, heck, threw one for yourself? Do something different this week, and use the space here to plan it out and document your results!

Things I did :DIFFERENT: this week:

_____

_____

_____

_____

_____

_____

DAY 4

DAY 5

By now, I am guessing these first few days feel like a LOT. There's been a lot of putting yourself out there, fighting your comfort zone, and facing unknowns. If you're a normal, sane person, this is hard stuff to do! Especially if you're flexing fear muscles that you have rarely used.

For today's challenge, I am going to ask you to get vulnerable with yourself and explore how all this is going. What are the excuses you've found yourself making? Have you pushed through them, or are there some that diverted your plans? If you didn't go as BIG and splashy with these first few challenges, why not? What was stopping you, and how can we clear those roadblocks for the next ninety-five days so you can hit harder, grow bigger, and face more?

DAY 6

Looking at your excuses and routine drags more closely, let's dig in on one of my favorite tricks to get beyond the hesitation, dread, and annoyance we have with everyday items in our routine. Let's take you from "I have to" to "I get to!"

This is a simple trick that immediately helps change perspective and create a mindset of gratitude and excitement. Simply change "I have to" to "I get to," "I choose to," or "I'm blessed to."

"I have to travel for work" ↝ "I'm blessed to travel for work"

"I have to help my kids with their schoolwork" ↝ "I get to help my kids with their schoolwork"

"I have to plan my partner's birthday" ↝ "I choose to plan my partner's birthday"

I challenge you to take a list of your excuses and time sucks and reframe them from "I have to" to whatever is most appropriate. In the final column, list the positive moments and recognize the little joys that come from traveling or working with your kids on a project. For "I choose to," identify why it is an awesome choice for you to plan an epic birthday, or if you don't "have to" choose to do that, identify how you can outsource, simplify, or change up that task!

Tasks/Excuses I "HAVE TO"	Reframed I "GET TO" / "CHOOSE TO" / "AM BLESSED TO"	"This shift ALLOWS ME to..."

DAY 7

In exploring my fears and obstacles, I was often asked what my REAL biggest fear was, and for me, that was losing someone I loved. I decided to write a *very* honest letter to my parents (who are both alive and in good health) to not only tell them how much I appreciate them but also let them know the things I'd like to change in our relationship to make the best of all our time together on earth. This letter changed my relationship with my parents and still has to this day. My dad, who had a hard time expressing feelings with words, has become the most loving dad I could ask for. And my mom, who is normally pretty anxious, has become far more optimistic around me.

For today's challenge, write an honest letter to the person you care about most to tell them, first and foremost, how much you appreciate them and the force of good they are in your life. Second, note all the ways you'd like to take advantage of the years you get to spend together. How can you combine your forces for good? What things would you like to work on together to change things for the better?

TO:

DAY 8

One acronym that I particularly love to celebrate is YOLO (you only live once)! Living like it's your last day on earth can bring you a fresh sense of honesty and really help you prioritize your goals. To that end, what is something you enjoy doing that you do not share with the world? What's stopping you from sharing?

Do you love to write, but only in a journal? Sing, but only in the shower? Dance in your kitchen, doodle in a private notebook, cook, paint, or give pep talks just for yourself?

Whatever it may be, do it like no one is watching. **I challenge you to tap into something you love and share it with the world.** Perhaps you could write a post about it so more people know about it!

I love to:

♡ _____

♡ _____

♡ _____

♡ _____

♡ _____

I'm going to share that that _love_ by:

- ♡ _____
- ♡ _____
- ♡ _____
- ♡ _____
- ♡ _____
- ♡ _____
- ♡ _____
- ♡ _____
- ♡ _____
- ♡ _____
- ♡ _____

DAY 9

Who here loves to create to-do lists? That's not what this challenge is about. Today, you're going to take some time to brag about yourself.

I challenge you to start an "I did it!" list! Write down some of your biggest accomplishments, moments, and milestones from the last year!

I DID IT!

- ☑ _____
- ☑ _____
- ☑ _____
- ☑ _____
- ☑ _____
- ☑ _____
- ☑ _____
- ☑ _____
- ☑ _____

- [ ] _____
- [ ] _____
- [ ] _____
- [ ] _____
- [ ] _____
- [ ] _____
- [ ] _____
- [ ] _____
- [ ] _____
- [ ] _____
- [ ] _____
- [ ] _____
- [ ] _____
- [ ] _____

You're remarkable! Looking at this list, do you feel remarkable? You've accomplished so much! I know we are always looking for more, to grow and always be better, but let's take a moment this week to reflect on how amazing you are and what all these accomplishments have in common.

DAY 10

OMG! You're 10 percent done with this challenge! How are you feeling? We've tackled your fears, goals, excuses, passions, and accomplishments! I'm so excited for you to dig in and keep striving for growth as we move out of part 1 and on to part 2!

As we look to the next phase of the journey, I challenge you to take a beat to pause and celebrate life. Write down twenty-five wonderful things you've experienced, including during the last ten days! For example, having an ice cream on a summer day, finding cash in your pocket, loving someone who loves you back, kissing your baby's tummy, watching the sunrise, reading an amazing book...whatever makes you feel bliss! Whatever moments in life leave you feeling grateful, leave you feeling alive and saying YES...which is what these first ten days have been all about.

1. _____
2. _____
3. _____
4. _____
5. _____
6. _____
7. _____
8. _____

9. _____
10. _____
11. _____
12. _____
13. _____
14. _____
15. _____
16. _____
17. _____
18. _____
19. _____
20. _____
21. _____
22. _____
23. _____
24. _____
25. _____

TWO

hello, ~~fearless~~ BRAVE.

> ## HOW TO INFLUENCE PEOPLE POSITIVELY

In the Hello, Fears book, this chapter is about becoming an influencer and choosing brave over fearless.

DAY 11

As we explore chapter 2 in the *Hello, Fears* book, you'll see that there is a big, BIG difference between fearless and brave!

Lacking fear is something I don't believe to be possible. But showing courage? That's where the magic happens. By owning our bravery, we are owning how courageous we are! Being brave is when we have the courage to take action despite the fear, and that is way more inspiring than being fearless!

I challenge you to look at those in your life you admire, particularly those who make brave choices that inspire you. List them, along with how they inspire you! If you're brave enough after doing so, send them a quick text or even call them, letting them know how much you admire and appreciate them! Or simply share a photo of this list with them!

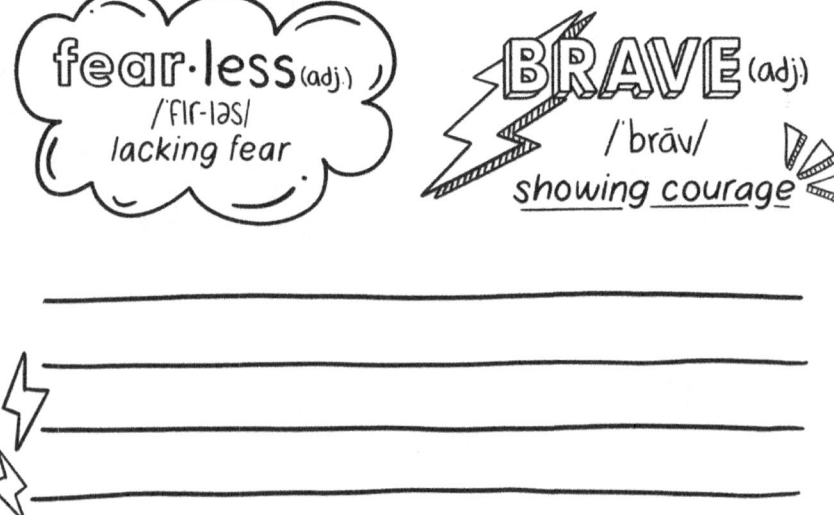

DAY 12

Fear can be very personal. I recently discovered that some people around me never considered me a fearful person in the first place. In fact, from their perspective I was considered a "brave girl."

Turns out that the two people who brought this to my attention suffer from slight social anxiety, and I've always been a social butterfly. As I considered myself a fearful teenager, I had no idea that close friends considered me courageous.

On the other hand, I consider my best friend extremely brave! She willingly divorced her husband to find herself and then she traveled solo all around Europe. For me, the solo traveling would be terrifying in itself. Not to mention the divorce! But for her, it was liberating.

Courage is relative!

Have you ever thought about in which areas of your life you would consider yourself to be fearless, in which areas you'd say you're fearful, and in which ones you're brave?

This week's challenge is simple enough on its face! Write down some areas of your life for each category.

fearful	fearless	Brave

DAY 13

After yesterday, you should have some categories and aspects of your life sorted between fearless, fearful, and brave. (And if you skipped yesterday, flip back and do it now!)

For today's challenge, I want you to ask two people who are close to you to help you answer the same question. I know, I know! Not necessarily an easy ask. Just keep in mind that getting vulnerable with loved ones is in itself an act of bravery. Ask them in which areas of life they consider you to be fearless, fearful, and brave.

What about their answers surprised you? Do you feel like you are in complete alignment, or did you learn something new by seeing yourself through their eyes?

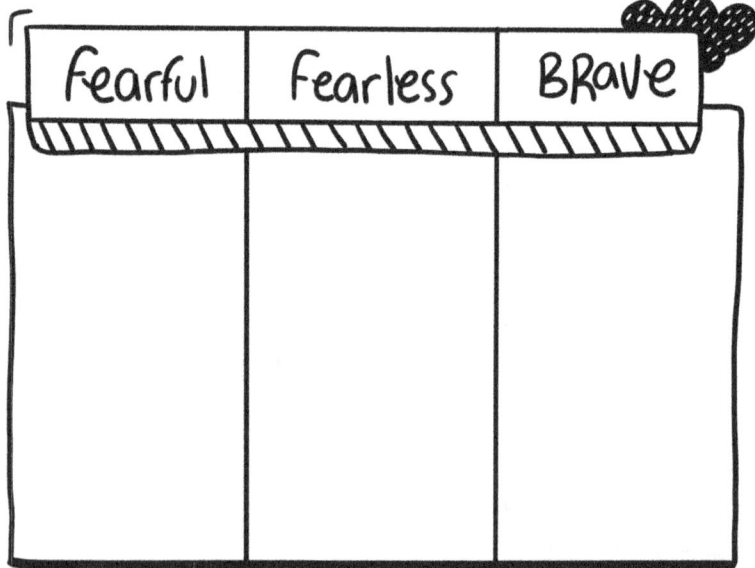

Fearful	Fearless	Brave

DAY 14

Now that we are moving forward in bravery, let's look at impact! After talking to your loved ones, what does your final column look like?

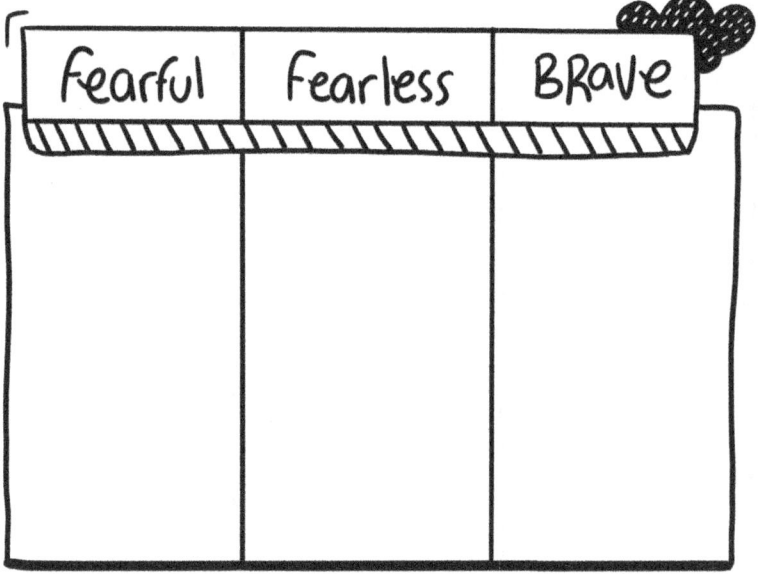

How does your fearless column impact your fearful column, and how do both relate to your brave column? How can we move more fearful items into brave or even fearless?

Today, I challenge you to examine your final list and pick something from your fearful column that you're going to recategorize. How you get there is up to you, but you can plan your next steps on the next page!

DAY 15

What does leadership mean to you? So many view leaders as those in high-level positions inspiring change, whereas leaders are often those I see showing *everyday leadership*. For example, my brother Daniel is a film director, and he is constantly sharing with me his new tricks to edit engaging videos. And I listen. My aunt Doris loves to share all the tips she's collected on how to live a healthier life. And I listen! These people influence my daily life and make it way better. In fact, they influence me way more than the so-called influencers on social media.

This is what I call *everyday leadership*. You don't need to have a certain title, award, or following to be intentional when it comes to influencing those you care about and beyond. But sadly, not everybody is willing to share their knowledge. Some people don't trust their worth—they assume that everybody already knows everything and that their thoughts are not original enough to share.

Well, today, I challenge you to think about leadership. Who are YOU as a leader? Write down a list of things you're good at—the things people always ask you for advice about. Perhaps you know all about traveling, good food in your area, cooking, music, makeup, fashion, sustainability, mental health... What is it?

DAY 16

Today, we are going to further explore your value as an everyday leader. The world needs YOUR value. Is your contribution less than perfect? More importantly, did it help you? Then perfect or not, it will help others. The truth is that you may not know it all, but I bet you can think of three people who might benefit from your approach. And if three can, three hundred can too.

I challenge you to look at the list you made yesterday and pick one to SHARE! It's time to help others grow. Start with some loved ones and see what the impact can be!

DAY 17

Like my brother Daniel and my aunt Doris, we are all surrounded by who I call *everyday leaders*. Maybe there was a doorman who once taught you a lesson about gratefulness, or your eighth grade teacher who believed in your artistic skills. Everyday leaders are truly all around us!

Today, I challenge you to make a list of forty people who have influenced your life positively in one way or another. I know, I know, forty sounds like a LOT, but trust me, it is not!

1. _____   11. _____
2. _____   12. _____
3. _____   13. _____
4. _____   14. _____
5. _____   15. _____
6. _____   16. _____
7. _____   17. _____
8. _____   18. _____
9. _____   19. _____
10. _____   20. _____

21. _____
22. _____
23. _____
24. _____
25. _____
26. _____
27. _____
28. _____
29. _____
30. _____
31. _____
32. _____
33. _____
34. _____
35. _____
36. _____
37. _____
38. _____
39. _____
40. _____

DAY 18

Traditional gender roles say that men are big, strong, and brave and that women are meek, protected, and submissive. I'm ashamed to say that for most of my young life, I was actively relieved that I was able to hide behind my fears, all tied up in my role as a girl instead of having to be brave like the boys!

I challenge you to explore any boundaries that are keeping you within traditional gender roles. Afraid of being too loud, too outspoken? Too selfish if you aren't putting everyone else in your life first? There are limits we all place upon ourselves that go unchecked. Don't allow any assigned to your gender to get in your way.

DAY 19

While I may have leaned in to being fearful and submissive as a young girl, as I have learned and grown, I've realized what so many have before me: being a woman is NOT an excuse to stay in the comfort zone. It's a reason to get out of it.

Looking at yourself as an everyday leader, how can you influence other women positively? **I challenge you to look at the strong and perhaps not-strong-YET women in your life, and see how you can support them and help them join you in this GROWTH revolution!**

DAY 20

As we wrap up your first twenty challenges, the BEST tool I can leave you with is the challenge to document your small (and not-so-small) acts of courage! Use this as a running list to track your BRAVERY! Big or small, whenever you face a fear and achieve a small win, track it here! You never know whom you'll leave inspired with your courage.

Today, I challenge you to kick off your list with your first act of courage! You got this!

THREE
hello, SOCIETY

> **CHECKING YOUR OWN BOXES**

In the Hello, Fears book, this chapter is about figuring out what to do with others' opinions and society's checklists.

DAY 21

I will kiss a boy when I turn fifteen. I will have my first serious boyfriend at seventeen. I will get married (to the same boyfriend) right after graduating from college. I will find a stable job in my preferred field, work there for a couple of years, and then have children when I'm twenty-five or twenty-six…no, twenty-five! We will live happily ever after. End of story.

Do you, or did you, also have a mental checklist with milestones and the appropriate ages for each one? I sure did! My personal example was imperfect, which we'll explore tomorrow, but it certainly got me thinking about my life and goals!

For today's challenge, create your own life checklist. You can put goals on it you've already been able to check and also those you are still missing. This list should include those goals you feel you are expected to fulfill. Make sure to add an age next to each goal like I did.

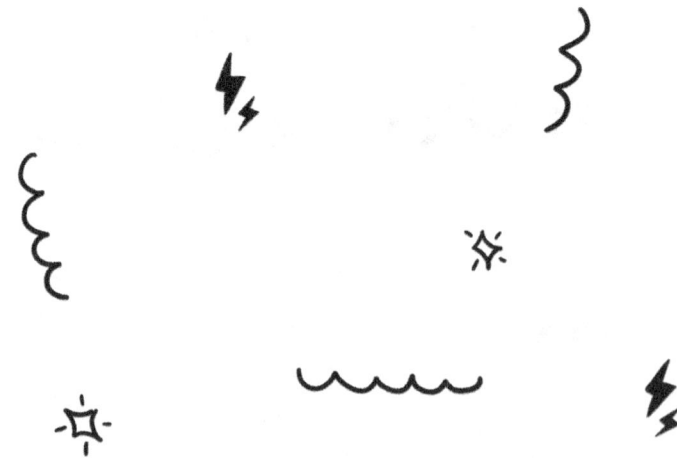

LIFE CHECKLIST

- [x] _____
- [x] _____
- [x] _____
- [x] _____
- [x] _____
- [x] _____
- [x] _____
- [x] _____
- [x] _____
- [x] _____
- [x] _____
- [x] _____
- [x] _____
- [x] _____

- [ ] _____
- [ ] _____
- [ ] _____
- [ ] _____
- [ ] _____
- [ ] _____
- [ ] _____
- [ ] _____
- [ ] _____
- [ ] _____
- [ ] _____
- [ ] _____
- [ ] _____
- [ ] _____

DAY 22

When it came to my own personal life checklist, I mostly followed it! That is until after a few months of being married when I suddenly had my first panic attack. I realized that I was almost done with the checklist I had made up for my life, and what was left wasn't enough!

I had started to feel uncomfortable with so much comfort around me. My life was stable and expected, and it suddenly felt monotonous! That was when it hit me: most people tend to seek comfort, not happiness—two things that can be easily confused. For some, comfort is happiness: the more comfortable they are and the less challenged they feel, the happier they believe they are.

Let's revise your life checklist. What's on it that is making you HAPPY? What's on it that you feel is there only to bring you COMFORT? **Today's challenge: add a few more things to your checklist, but this time, focus on things that would bring you genuine HAPPINESS.** Dare to dream BIG! Think of it this way: if you couldn't share those accomplishments or milestones with anybody, would they still make you happy? Many times, we want to achieve certain goals just to impress others, and that won't bring happiness in the end.

LIFE CHECKLIST | Happy | Comfortable

DAY 23

In my personal journey, our revised checklist ended up bringing my husband and I to New York so we could explore becoming entrepreneurs in the city that never sleeps! However, those in our support network couldn't understand what the heck we were doing! They were confused as to why were we leaving our community when the next logical step was for us to get a mortgage and start making babies? How could we abandon *the plan*?

Which need are you trying to satisfy: the need to fit in for others or the need to pursue your own path? Looking at your checklist, who can you rely on for support? Who may (from a place of love) try to hinder your goals? **Today, I challenge you to explore both groups and plan to ask for help (you're going to need it) and for understanding (while they'll understand when they see you happy, it's best to address things ASAP).**

Go to for support

Roadblock to address

DAY 24

The best way to ask for help is by knowing ourselves and what we need. People try to help from their own perspective, and they like to do for others what they would like others to do for them. That rarely works! 😖

If we want to help others, we need to know what THEY need. It may be vastly different from what we'd like. For example, Adam's happy sheet might be the complete opposite to mine and say things like:

Adam's happy Sheet:
I need alone time
Don't ask me how I feel every 10 min.
Give me a home-cooked meal

Mine is all about: presence, quality time, Matcha Latte, Company, Takeout Sushi, words of AFFIRMATION

Today's challenge is necessary! Write down a list of things that always make you feel better emotionally (a hug, walks down the beach, the sunset, an iced latte, words of affirmation). Then, write another list including all the things that make you feel worse (lack of empathy, attention, or understanding; being told what to do and how to feel). This list is not for you to keep but for you to SHARE. Your loved ones need to know how to help you when you need them the most. Ask them to do the same and share it with you so you can be there for them when they need you. I call this my #happysheet because...sheet happens!

DAY 25

Think about the choices you've made in your life to satisfy others' expectations. Perhaps it was your career choice, the school you graduated from, the person you married (or divorced), the job you go to every day, the number of children you have, the way you look, the city you live in, the car you drive. Which of those choices were made to satisfy you, and which ones were to satisfy others, society perhaps?

Take three things about your life that you once chose in order to fit in, make someone else happy, or be liked (be as honest as possible with yourself here). Note not just what they are, but why you are doing them.

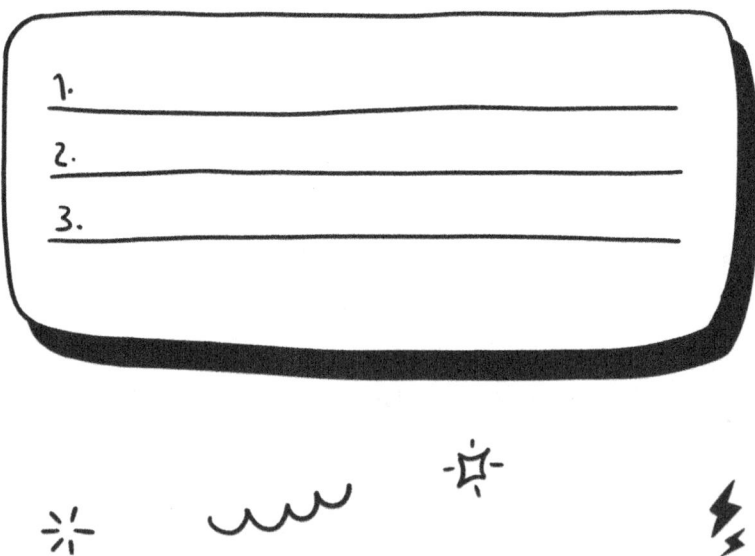

1. _____
2. _____
3. _____

Now, list three things about your life that you once chose to make YOURSELF happy. As with before, note not just what they are, but what about doing them makes you feel happy!

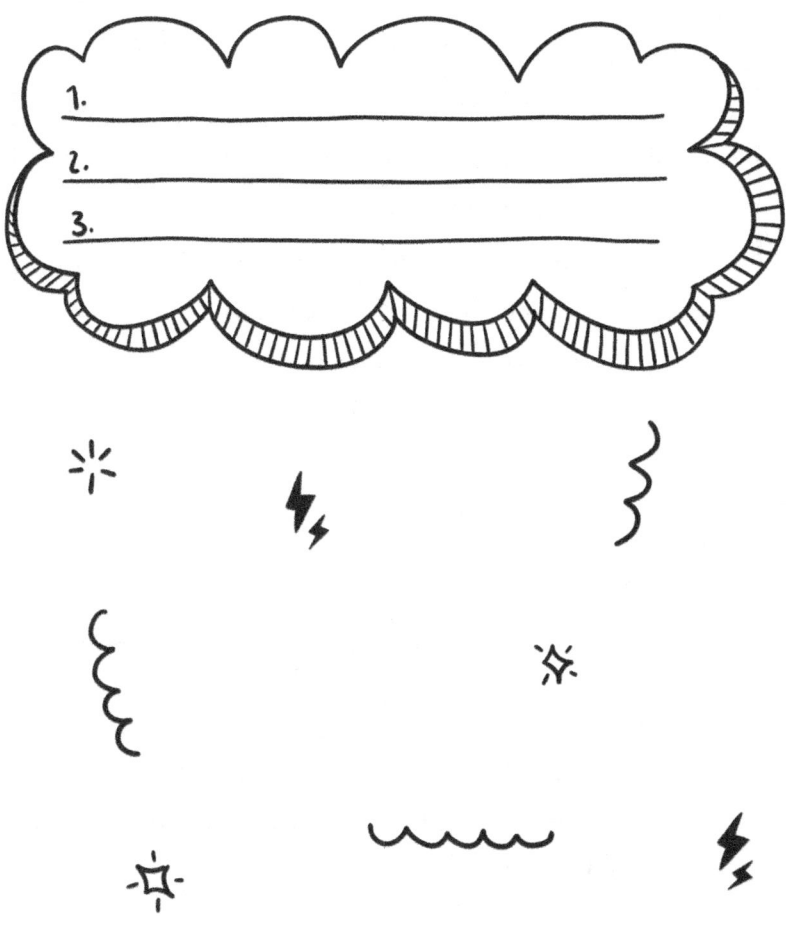

DAY 26

Making choices for yourself versus for others is always hard, especially when there are so many expectations that surround them to reckon with. Let's do a quick exercise. Respond with your immediate reaction and circle the phrase that applies:

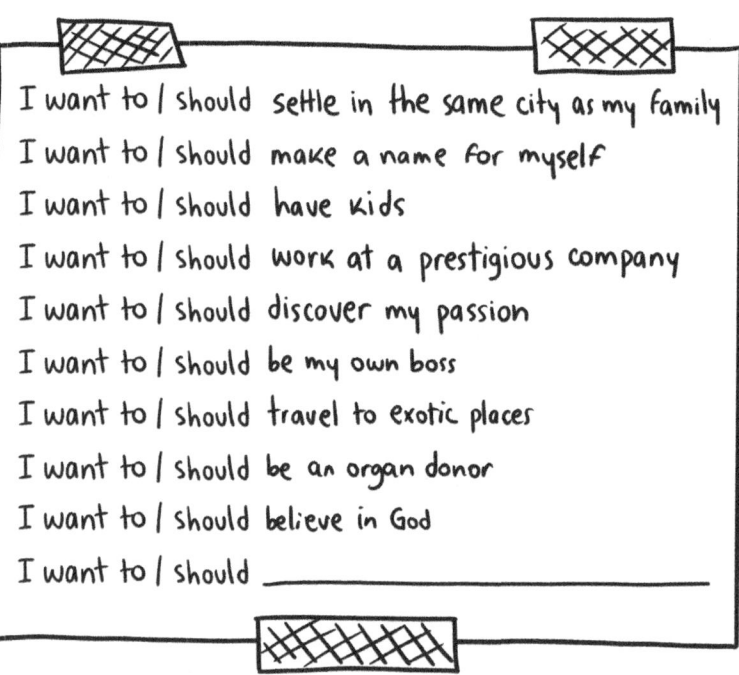

I want to / should settle in the same city as my family
I want to / should make a name for myself
I want to / should have kids
I want to / should work at a prestigious company
I want to / should discover my passion
I want to / should be my own boss
I want to / should travel to exotic places
I want to / should be an organ donor
I want to / should believe in God
I want to / should _____

Looking at your immediate reactions, did you find any surprises? **Today, pick one and explore how your choice affects you moving forward.**

DAY 26

DAY 27

If there is one thing I hope you're taking away from this portion of the challenge, it's that you should never, ever settle. While you may need to make sacrifices for your goals, including doing things you don't want to do or making choices that are less than ideal, they should all be in the name of accomplishing YOUR dreams.

The things you will value most in your life are the things you are going to want for yourself. **Today's challenge is simple: what is one thing about your life that you feel you settled for?** Is this something you'd like to change? In that case, what steps do you need to take to follow a different path, one that is more aligned to your personal goals? It's okay if this endeavor can take up to five or ten years. You don't need to accomplish all your dreams TODAY.

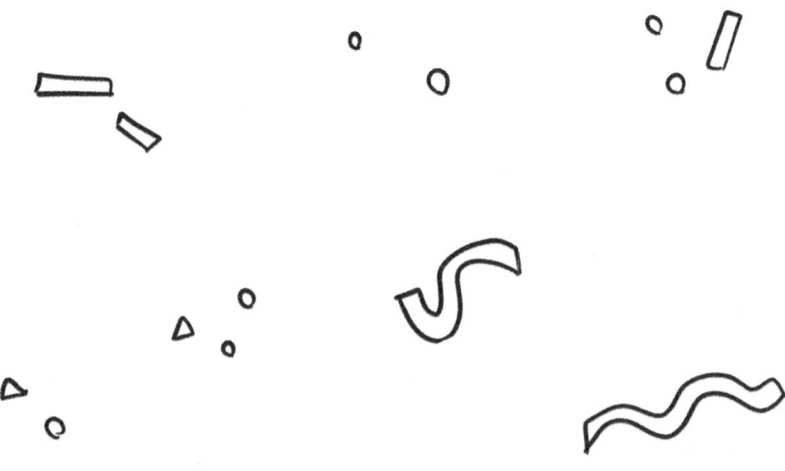

DAY 28

Abraham Maslow is the famous psychologist who came up with Maslow's hierarchy of basic needs. Remember that pyramid? Here's what one looks like for me:

It all starts at the bottom, with our basic needs—air, water, and food (specifically ramen with a soft-boiled egg if you're like me). Then you work your way up to your ideal shelter, then being a part of your community and having a sense of tribe, of belonging. Next up is having a positive self-esteem before we finally get to self-actualization.

Today's challenge: complete your own pyramid. Maslow claimed if we don't satisfy our basic needs, we can never reach the top. Start with your base and move upward. Are you set up for success?

DAY 29

To get where I am today involved a LOT of sacrifice. Mostly, I had to give up my old self to become who I wanted to be. But my choices upended my ENTIRE life, especially when I took a look at where I was and essentially redid everything. (Well, almost everything. Adam is still my hubby! But even our relationship took a leap for the best.)

Today, look at opportunities to redo. Answer the following questions for yourself, as always, being as authentic and honest with yourself as humanly possible!

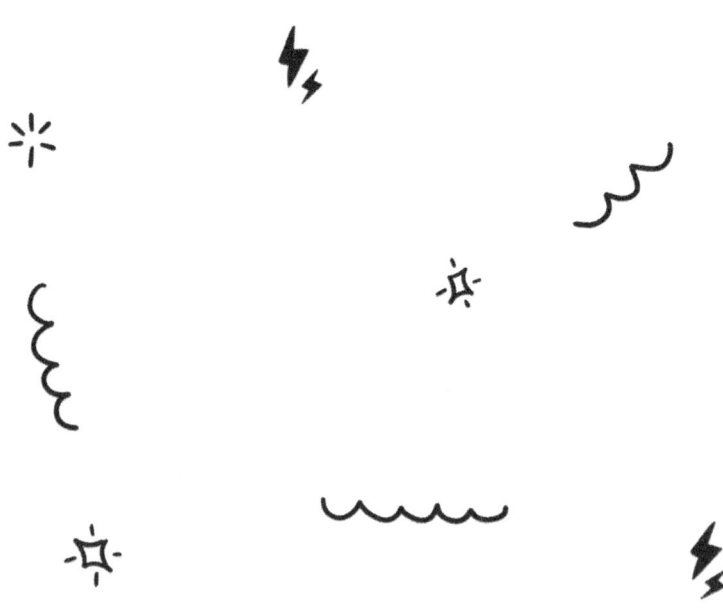

DAY 30

Reviewing your answers from yesterday's four questions, have any of your answers already come true? If not, what is the very first, tiny step you can take to make some of those dreams a reality?

Using the lines on the next page, write out if you've already accomplished these goals (in other words, you are living exactly in the world where you want to!) or those first small steps you can take toward living your best life!

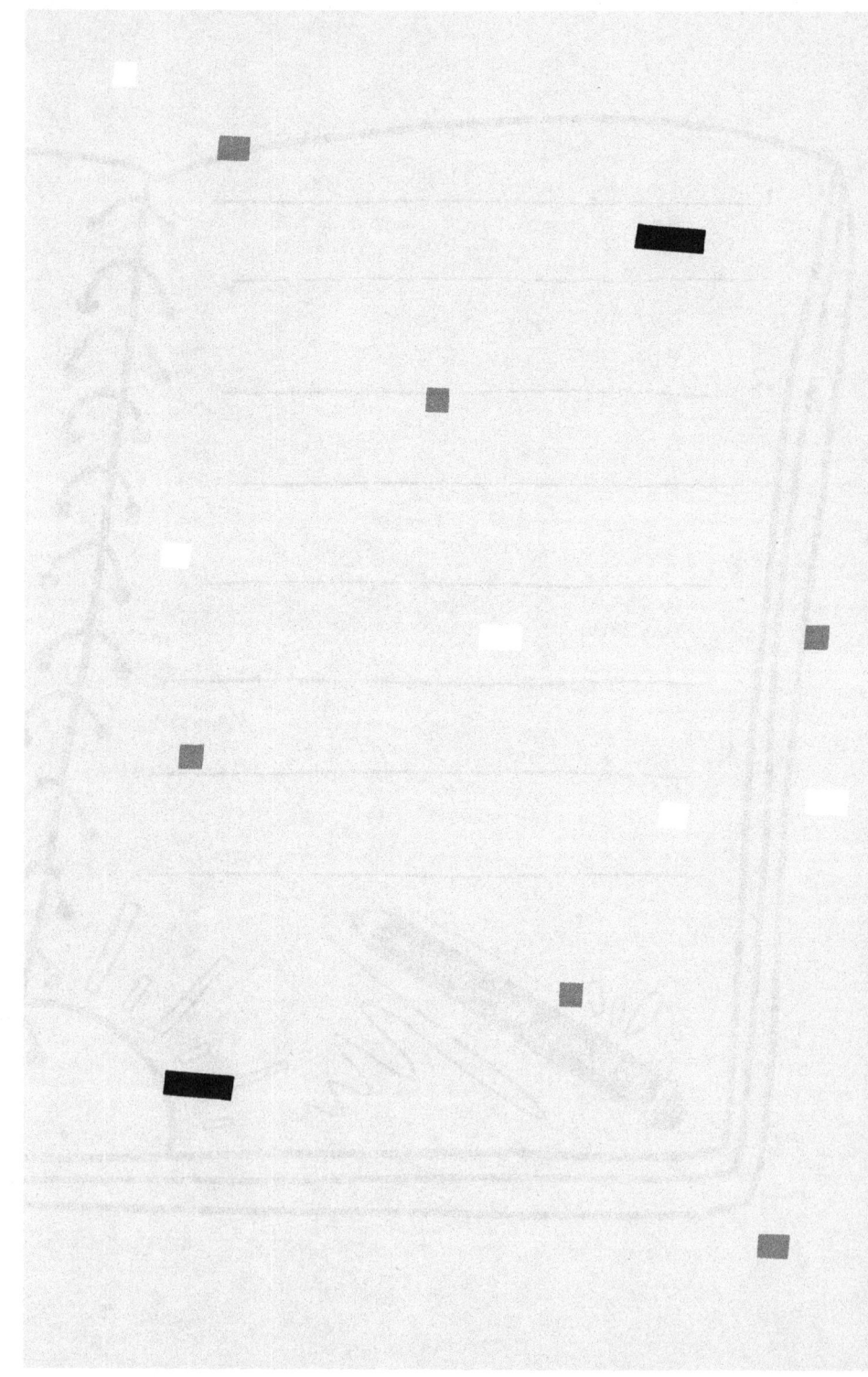

FOUR

hello, YOU

BECOMING YOUR AUTHENTIC SELF

In the Hello, Fears book, this chapter is about self-branding and overcoming impostor syndrome.

DAY 31

Congratulations! We are starting a new section of the challenge, AND you've made it through a month of exploring your fears and getting REAL with your goals! I'm proud of you!

Today, we are going to start working on your personal brand. How can you be more intentional about it so others perceive you exactly in the way you'd like to be perceived?

So for today's challenge, I want you to identify your nonnegotiable values. Identifying our values helps us become more intentional with our actions. For example, I can't say that I'm detail-oriented if I never give my mom, my BFF, or my lovely coworker gifts on their birthdays. Wanting to be something is not enough; we need to identify the kind of person we want to be and take action!

From this list, identify the ten values that best represent you in the NOW.

Now circle three to four that are the MOST important values for you.

Show the full list of values to three people who are very close to you. Ask them to identify the three main values that you represent and see if they chose the same ones you did for yourself.

Go back to the list and choose one aspirational value, something you wish you could embody one day. (In my case, I chose "courageous" in 2015 before starting my fear-facing journey.)

VALUES

Accuracy	Authenticity	Adventure	Balance
Simplicity	Collaboration	Connection	Compassion
Courage	Creativity	Discipline	Excellence
Ethics	Faith	Freedom	Friendship
Happiness	Thoughtfulness	Health	Humor
Integrity	Justice	Style	Love
Gratitude	Family	Loyalty	Passion
Power	Security	Stability	Transparency
Wealth	Accountability	Community	Diversity
Equality	Honesty	Empathy	Fun
Inclusivity	Respect	Selflessness	Optimism

1. _____   2. _____   3. _____

My Aspirational Value: _____

DAY 31

DAY 32

One very common mistake that we all make is that we compare ourselves to others very often. Since we were children, we have been taught to look around as a way to discover who we are. From the moment we're born, people compare us to our parents ("You have your mom's eyes and your dad's charm"), then to our cousins, friends, classmates, coworkers...

Today, your challenge is to CONTRAST. To do that, I want you to write down a list of people you always compare yourself to in all walks of life (as an employee/entrepreneur/student, as a daughter, as a friend, as a mom, as a spouse, etc.).

Then, write one to two things that set you apart from those people, things you have and they don't.

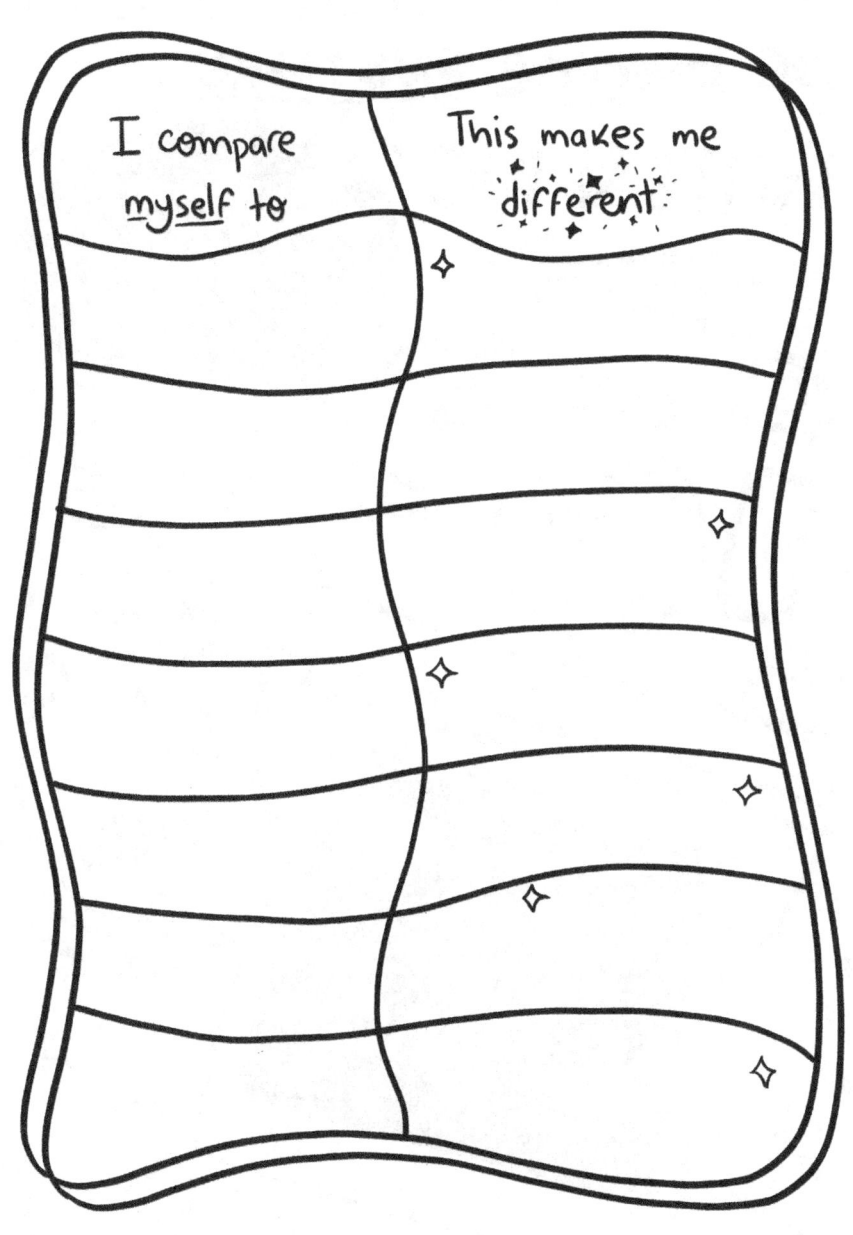

WHEN WE COMPARE WE become ONE MORE

WHEN WE CONTRAST WE BECOME

One OF a Kind

DAY 32

DAY 33

My mom is the one who taught me about the idea of living life authentically versus perfectly. She taught me that we can either embrace or despise our "imperfections," but when we highlight our authentic selves in a positive light, others will also see the beauty in us. She taught me about Frida Kahlo and her bushy eyebrows—*before* bushy eyebrows were a thing—Cindy Crawford and her upper lip mole, and Cher with her deep, contralto voice.

That's right, I credit my mom with my first personal branding lesson!

Today's challenge is to identify one thing you may not like about yourself but that is a by-product of what makes you great and unique. For example, Adam considers himself slow because he takes his time to do his work, which frustrates him. Being slow is a by-product of being strategic, intentional, and organized. In my case, some people think I am self-centered, which is a by-product of being confident and always pursuing my own dreams.

What I don't like about my personality is:

↓ This is a BY-PRODUCT of my: ↓

_____
_____
_____
_____
_____
_____
_____
_____

The things we don't like about ourselves are **BY-PRODUCTS** of the things that MAKE US Great

DAY 33

DAY 34

To put our authentic selves forward, we need to surround ourselves with communities who will fully embrace us.

Today, look to your tribe. Do you notice that you act or feel differently when you surround yourself with different groups of people? I know I do! Explore the following three categories:

Enemies — While not always overt, some people around us just bring out the worst in us! Personally, I go from happy and uplifting to pissed and entitled when I am around the particular toxic group that comes to mind. Who is this group for you? These are not real enemies, just your authentic self enemies. Makes sense? You are not yourself around these people.

_____
_____
_____
_____
_____

Frenemies These are friends and loved ones I may find super cool, but I realize when I am around them that I feel a certain pressure to show off or seem more confident than I really am! That's so exhausting and makes me question my own worth. <u>Who makes you wonder if you are enough?</u>

_____

_____

_____

_____

≋FRIENDS≋ With my all-time BFFs and close family is where I feel 100% ME, 100% of the time. <u>Who are the star players in that group for you?</u>

_____

_____

_____

_____

DAY 35

My professor at the School of Visual Arts, Dr. Tom Guarriello, shared with us a famous quote from poet Muriel Rukeyser: "The Universe is made of stories, not of atoms." The truth is that we can all be saying the same things at the same time, but what will resonate with people is not necessarily the content itself but the way we share it.

Telling your story is the last thing you have to take into account when sharing your most authentic self with the world in your most authentic voice. It's not about what you share, it's about how you share it. Do you know how many people are talking about fear right now? Way too many, but none of them discuss it in the exact same way I do.

What's your story? Today, I challenge you to write it out and then share it with someone you love!

DAY 36

Accepting ourselves is no easy ask, and for most of us, even when we begin to accomplish goals, we still don't feel like we are successful. This is when something called impostor syndrome will pop up. It means exactly what it sounds like: that despite success, we feel like failures or undeserving of our accomplishments. It creates a cycle that looks something like this:

Are you stuck in your own impostor syndrome loop? Try your hand at identifying your own unhealthy cycle—it can be with work, health, personal goals, or even your family! Where do you feel undeserving or like you aren't finding success? Chances are you ARE and just need to pause to recognize it!

DAY 37

Especially if we're high achievers, it is so easy to feel like an impostor when we take note of all the other high achievers in our lives. They are accomplishing their goals, and we see them as smarter, funnier, more good looking, harder working, you name it! The truth is, though, that we can see everyone else's attributes but rarely see our own.

I know you love criticizing yourself and finding every flaw. I love picking myself apart too. **But for this next exercise, I challenge you to do the opposite.** Take five minutes and write out as many remarkable things about yourself as you can in the space provided! These are things you practice often that make you feel proud of yourself on a daily basis, not once-in-a-lifetime achievements.

These are some of my answers

I'm REMARKABLE because:
- I love life
- I work daily on maintaining a healthy marriage
- I made it in a foreign country
- I seek criticism as a way to grow
- I accept myself as I am

I'm Remarkable because...

_____
_____
_____
_____
_____
_____
_____
_____
_____
_____

DAY 38

Self-acceptance is when we make the decision to embrace those things we can't change about ourselves and that we may not like. Some of the things I wish were different about me are the fact that I need glasses to see the world, my insane number of moles and freckles, my low pain threshold, and my short stature. But those things, along with the ones I do like about myself, come together to make me one whole and real person. Meanwhile, self-love is when you want to become the best version of yourself, so you get uncomfortable to make it happen! Like when we exercise, choose to eat healthier food, go to therapy, learn a new skill...

Today, let's explore both!

self-acceptance — What is one thing about yourself that you are willing to accept? How does it feed into you as a whole, amazing package? _____
_____
_____
_____
_____

self-love — What is one thing about yourself you'd like to improve in the following months? How will it help you grow? _____
_____
_____
_____
_____

DAY 39

Your unique selling proposition (USP) is the one thing that sets you apart from the rest, and this is something I learned during my advertising days. Whenever we were assigned to sell a product or a service, the first thing we had to identify was the USP: What about this product or service does the client want us to highlight? What does it provide that no other product can?

Have you thought about what your USP is? If you have more than one, even better! Sometimes it can be a combination of things that when put together define exactly what makes you different.

For example, if I were to define my USP, I would say: *Michelle is an international keynote speaker with a fresh approach and a unique story. Her engaging presentation will have the entire room taking photos of her colorful slides, laughing at her self-deprecating but oh-so-relatable videos, and taking note of the unexpected life lessons she shares from the time she decided to turn her life upside down by going after her fears.*

As you can see here, I use very specific adjectives to describe who I am, what I do, how I do it, and why I do it. **Today, I challenge you to do the same! What's your USP?**

DAY 40

The best way to get to know ourselves better is to spend more time with ourselves!

Today, I challenge you to go on a date with yourself! This is a special date, not just any date. Where would you like to go? What would you like to do, eat, reflect upon? Perhaps you could go to the movie theater and then go for ice cream, or visit a nice rooftop to watch the sunrise and then have dinner. I did this for my birthday—I spent the entire day by myself and did all my favorite things in NYC! I had a blast. Use the space right here to plan your perfect day and assign a date to it!

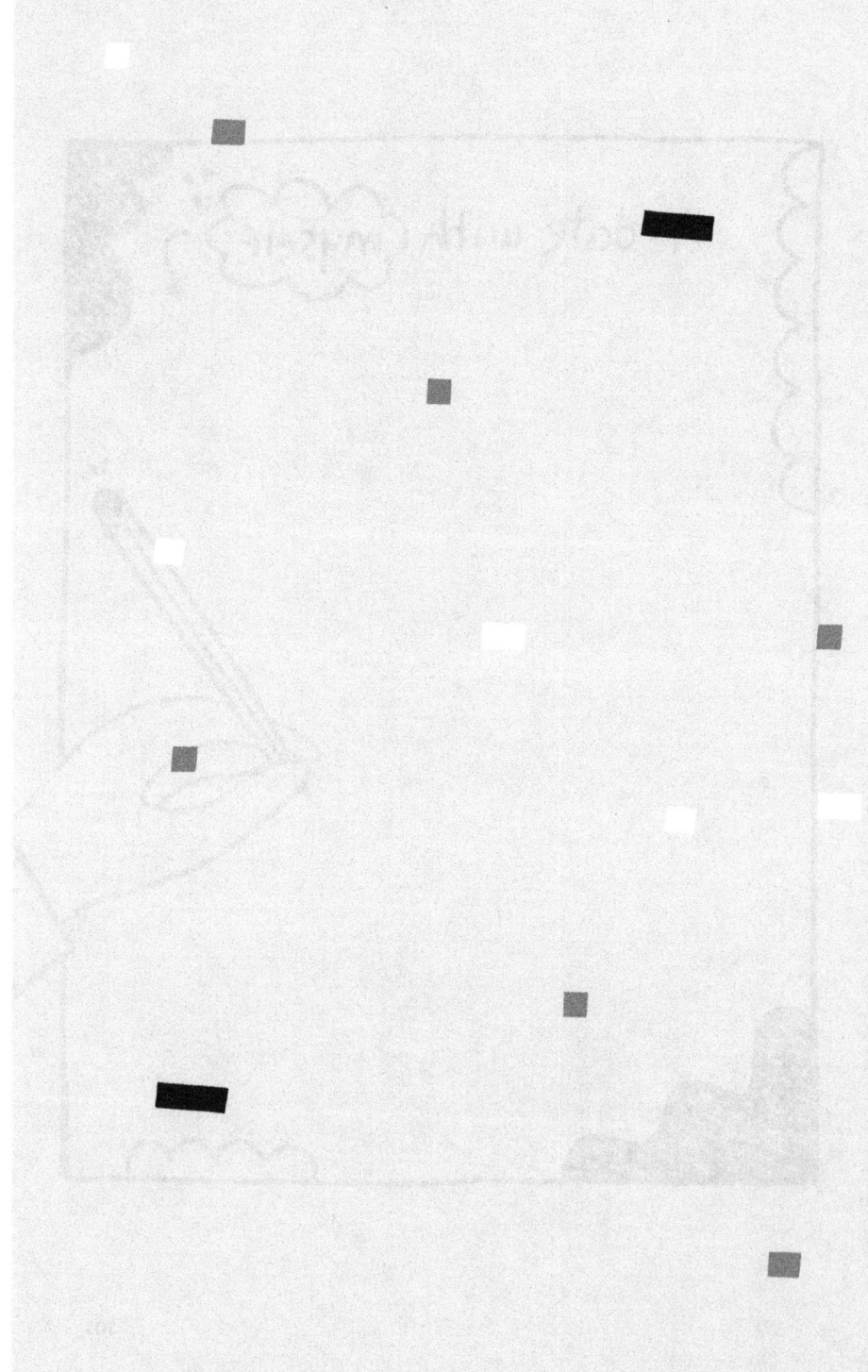

FIVE
hello, HATERS.

> **EXPOSING YOURSELF AND DEALING WITH CRITICISM**

In the Hello, Fears book, this chapter is about going viral and facing trolls.

DAY 41

At Day 44 of my personal 100-day project, I went viral and everything changed. My story became a wild, shared activity for readers ALL OVER THE GLOBE! I quickly realized as my inbox was flooded that the language of fear is universal.

Is going viral one of your dreams? What are those websites you'd love to be featured on? Or TV shows you'd like to be invited to? For one second, imagine that a project you create goes viral. **Now, use the space on the next page to describe how that would affect your life and how you would react to such surprise.**

The day I went viral...

DAY 42

One fun thing that happens when you go viral: the HATERS come out! Youth speaker A'ric Jackson has an interesting definition for haters:

Today, I'm challenging you with something far more difficult than calling out your own haters. I'm asking if YOU have ever been the hater. Have you ever been critical of a loved one's goals and dreams? Injected a dose of reality to someone's big plans, which may or may not have been necessary? Or even just been downright mean and negative with someone who came to you for support? Today's the day you own it and then work to make it up to them! It's never too late to show support, even if it is just in a text.

I messed up when I _____

and I plan to make amends by _____

DAY 43

While all of us might occasionally play the hater, trolls are in a whole different league of negativity. Trolls have practically made tearing others down into an art form. So the question becomes, how do we respond to intense, troll-level criticism?

Well, for myself, it drove me forward. Having gone viral, I had the experience of being midway through my fear challenge, reading live reactions. While reading messages about how I was a joke, not facing REAL fears, I decided that I was going to prove them wrong. They sparked a fire in me.

Today, I am going to challenge you to take one of those goals and dreams you've been workshopping and bring it to your biggest naysayer for feedback. Take all criticism in stride, and don't argue with your critic, but use their negativity to shine light on your weaknesses. Then prove them HELLA wrong.

After taking my (plans) to
_____

_____
_____
_____
_____
_____
_____,
I realized _____
_____
_____
_____
_____
_____

DAY 44

Now that you've faced a more literal troll in your life, it's time to face your INNER troll. We are all our biggest critics, and I am sure your inner troll has been champing at the bit to be released to let you know how silly this whole challenge and all your dreams are!

Today, I challenge you to talk to your troll and get it all out. Give your troll a nickname, hear out the biggest comments your troll has for you, and then refute them. This is a two-sided conversation that I am sure you'll come out on top of!

Hello, _____, my personal troll! Let's hear your troll-i-est comments!

TROLL FEEDBACK:

Your BRILLIANT response:

DAY 44

DAY 45

Now that you've heard out your troll, it's time to forgive them and yourself for thinking such negative thoughts. The truth is that our inner trolls are the result of our stories, our upbringings, and our past experiences. Why do you think you talk to yourself in such a negative manner from time to time? Where does that come from?

Today, forgive your inner troll. It's not your fault, but we all have the responsibility to improve our self-talk. So after you forgive yourself, make a commitment to become more compassionate in your next opportunities. How do you feel?

Dear _____, (The name you gave your inner troll)

I forgive you for

_____
_____
_____
_____
_____

I promise to

_____
_____
_____
_____
_____

DAY 46

When negative comments or negative feedback is provided to us, we often want to flinch away and deny it. But it's always important to first ask ourselves, *Is it true?*

Whether from our trolls or naysayers, any feedback can be constructive. What are some negative comments you'd rather ignore than face? Guess what you're challenged to do today? 🙂

DAY 47

It can be hard on the ego to listen to negative comments, but as we learned yesterday, negative comments can help us grow.

Based on the feedback you exposed yesterday, come up with a plan to work on yourself or on those projects you have in mind and for which you've received either negative or constructive criticism. Sometimes, not receiving any feedback is also feedback! For example, if you have an Instagram account to talk about something you're passionate about or a product you sell, and no one is engaging with your content, how can you make it better?

_____

_____

_____

_____

_____

_____

_____

_____

_____

DAY 48

Once you expose yourself, the brave souls will take note, and we'll be there to support you. And one day, you will be there for those who are taking their first steps.

How can you support other brave souls around you? Can you share or promote what this person is doing? And if it's not quite developed enough, could you offer some advice and encouragement to them to keep trying or perhaps connect that person with the right mentor?

For today's challenge, put out a call on social media asking others how you can help support them! See what comes forward, and if you don't get anyone brave enough to bite, reach out directly to some loved ones with specific ways you'd love to support them! Recap how you make an impact in the space provided. When brave souls unite, well...good luck, haters.

DAY 49

When we dare to expose ourselves, we get extremely vulnerable, and that's freaking scary. *To be vulnerable is to be brave.* Because once we take the step and we are out there, anything can happen. We can triumph or we can fail, but either way, haters gonna hate.

A few days ago, you brought something vulnerable of yours forward to someone in your life who has been less than supportive, someone who came to mind when I was talking about trolls. **Today, I challenge you to thank them for allowing you to be vulnerable with them while also letting them know how hard it was for you given how they can respond.** Ideally, this will open them up to you as well, and perhaps you can share a vulnerable conversation about your relationship.

I got vulnerable with _____
_____
_____
_____!

And it went _____
_____
_____
_____
_____
_____
_____
_____
_____

DAY 50

While going viral invited trolls into my life, it also invited FANS! And more importantly for our fledging venture, sponsors. We were able to take on more expensive challenges and keep moving forward on the list of fears without continuing to spend our capital. As students living in New York, this was a GAME CHANGER! We had been nearing a point where we'd have to call it quits on the challenge and had been praying for solutions. Going viral provided us with the answer to our prayers! I call this speaking the language of the universe.

The universe does not always respond to prayers; it responds to positive actions. You want something, prove it. That's how I see it. The more uncomfortable you get, the more the universe listens.

Today, I challenge you to put forward your biggest prayer and flip it to action. What are your next steps? Time to map it out.

SIX
hello, EGO

UNLEARNING FAILURE

In the Hello, Fears book, this chapter is where I screw up my Netflix talk and tackle personal fears.

DAY 51

Holy COW, you're over halfway done! I hope you're feeling inspired and every challenge is cutting some of your self-limitations! As we move into the second half of this journey, we're going to be focusing on failure, so let's take a day to first celebrate your SUCCESS!

Fifty fear-focused days! Congratulations on taking such strides for yourself! **For today's challenge, let's go over your biggest wins since you started this journal.** What's been a big success for you, and how can we get more wins on the board as you enter the second half?

_____
_____
_____
_____
_____
_____
_____
_____
_____

DAY 52

As discussed in my book, failure, in my opinion, is not being unsuccessful but rather when we don't try at all. Most of us are so comfortable, we don't try to accomplish more. Whenever we try to hedge our bets or take a safer route to prevent failure, we are also preventing success.

It's that simple.

Today, I challenge you to explore what failures you're avoiding and thus what successes. For example, I was so afraid that no one would want to read my book, I didn't want to start to write it. Not trying would have prevented one of my biggest accomplishments to date!

FAILURES	SUCCESSES

DAY 53

Comfort often tells us things like "good things come to those who wait," but if you're reading this, then I bet you're like me and you're tired of waiting.

What's your first step to achieving your desired lifestyle and the success you envision for yourself? It may not be the exact right move, but I assure you ANY move is progress toward your goals.

Today's challenge is to take the first step toward a new dream. It could be as simple as doing some research about that dream, sketching out ideas, writing a list of to-dos, buying a book, or reaching out to someone who has already done something similar to what you want to accomplish.

my FIRST step toward my SUCCESS is...

DAY 53

the real enemy of **SUCCESS** is not *failure* it is actually COMFORT

DAY 54

Are you a dreamer or a doer? Dreamers are those who love to plan their perfect future lives. They can spend hours brainstorming and scribbling plans in their colorful dotted journals. They have pages filled with brilliant ideas, action steps, and rough-but-promising sketches. They have all the motivation but also all the excuses not to execute just yet!

Doers not only come up with dope ideas, they also execute them instead of waiting for others to make them happen. They don't believe in excuses or wait for the perfect moment. They know there is no such thing. They believe in the art of trying and failing and trying again.

Today, I challenge you to list all the excuses you tell yourself when you're about to turn your dreams into reality. Next to each excuse, I want you to write down what you can do about it to make your dreams come true! For example, "I don't have enough hours in the day" >> "I can wake up an hour early to make this happen" or "I will spend one hour less on social media."

Then, fill out beautifully the quote on page 136 and OWN it. You CAN become a DOER if you decide that's what you want. If I did it, you can too.

DAY 55

As you may have guessed, the difference between dreamers and doers is courage. As someone who loves to dream big (it's an awesome first step to success!), I love to surround myself with doers, as they help motivate me to spend less time dreaming and more time building.

Today's challenge has two parts. First, on the graph below, draw a black dot to mark where you stand right now in terms of dreaming and doing. Then draw a star where you want to be a few months from today. Add today's date on top of your dot and a desired date on top of your star to give yourself a deadline.

Second, take a picture of your personalized graph and share it on social media. Have your crew hold you accountable, and don't forget to tag us @hellofears!

DAY 56

Once you start making progress toward your goals, one of the most difficult aspects of failure can be rejection. After some particularly rough rejections, I started the #ShareTheWholeStory campaign on Instagram. Instagram has always been somewhere that shows you only the very best of your community's lives. When I publicly admitted some of the rejections I was processing, I was shocked at how many others were moved to share their own!

Sharing stories of vulnerability makes us realize we are not alone, and we all feel better keeping each other company. **So today, I challenge you to share your failures and rejection stories with others.** Ideally, you'll keep sharing beyond today, sharing as often as you share your wins. You will be surprised by how people react to vulnerability, and you will receive a ton of support when you need it the most.

> My most painful rejections were...

DAY 57

The biggest thing to keep in mind with hustle is that it is largely invisible. Most people only show *results* on social media or in stories they relay over cocktails, because the hustle to get to the result is not pretty or fun or entertaining. On the contrary, the hustle is slow, tedious, and full of baggy eyes, late nights, and empty coffee mugs. Who wants to see that?

Me! I do! And you should too! **Today, much like sharing your most painful rejections, share some of the steps and progress you're making toward your goals.** Though not glamorous, all the tiny steps toward progress are going to get you to your biggest "shares" yet!

Here is my #hustle! I'm moving forward and _____
_____
_____
_____
_____
_____
_____

DAY 58

The other important thing to keep in mind with rejection and failure is that NO success is overnight success. What may look like overnight success to you is actually years in the making. And if it were that easy, *everybody* would make it.

"How did you fail today?" is a question that Sara Blakely's dad used to ask her every night at the dinner table. Now the founder of Spanx—and one of the most influential and wealthiest women alive—Sara would eagerly tell her dad each day the amazing ways in which she tried but failed.

Your challenge for today is to FAIL! That's right! You need to try something you're not good at and fail. Trust me, you will learn so much just by failing. Write here what you failed at and what you learned from the experience.

Today I failed at:
_____
_____
_____
_____
_____

DAY 59

Social media can sometimes make us feel as if everybody is succeeding but us. But the truth is that everybody fails. Literally! That feeling can be challenging and discouraging for many. It is okay to unfollow those people and accounts that constantly make you feel as if you're not moving fast enough or working hard enough.

So today, I challenge you to list the accounts on social media that make you feel less worthy or capable....

Now, I challenge you to unfollow those people! You heard me right. Know that you can always follow them back again when you feel confident. If it's hurting you, why keep them close to you?

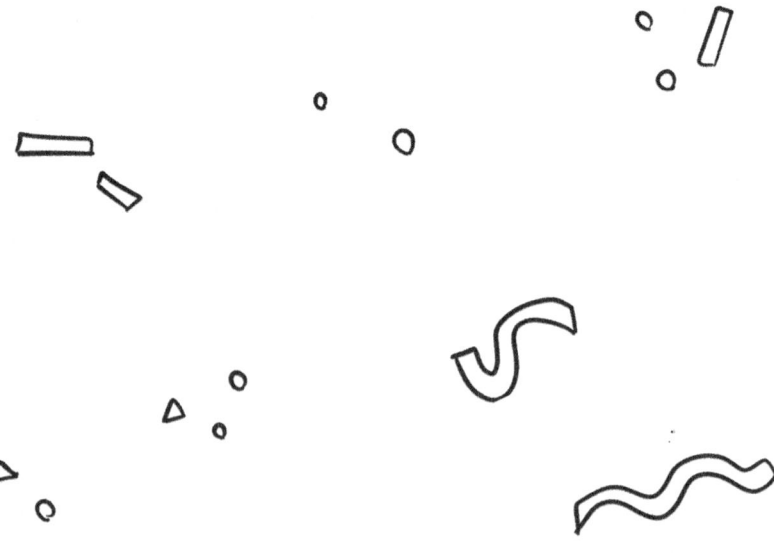

DAY 60

The best way to ensure we are overcoming failure is to choose action over perfection. Today, instead of asking "Why me?" let's reframe to ask "Why NOT me?" There's a lot on your plate, I know, because all of us are taking on so much and trying our best, and it is so easy to be thrown off and find ourselves adrift in self-pity. When you catch yourself saying "I can't do/become/create _____," change it up for "I can _____."

What CAN you do to move forward?

Today, I want you to turn some I can'ts into I cans! Your challenge is to rebrand and refocus your personal roadblocks into opportunities to move forward.

DAY 60

SEVEN
hello, GROWTH

> ## OVERCOMING THE WTF AM I DOING? STAGE

In the Hello, Fears book, this chapter is about Adam quitting his job and stepping forward into growth. Or as I like to call it, the most important chapter of my book!

DAY 61

Life will always give us choices: some will take us back into our comfort zone; others will challenge us, but help us grow. The important thing here is to identify which is the growth choice and choose that one despite the fear of what it may bring. In fact, that's the best way to tell them apart: growth is—most of the time—the scariest choice to make.

Look at a decision you have in front of you, one that can lead you to your next goal. It doesn't have to be as big as changing your whole career—it could even be a small decision that has the potential to help you become a better version of yourself. For example: *Should I ask him out? Move away from home? Accept that job offer? Try yoga? Buy a car? Eat healthier? Read that book?*

Once you've identified your "should I" question, write down the two choices you have regarding that decision. There may be more, but ultimately focus on the two biggest (yes or no)!

Now, circle and star the option that scares you the most. Keep that in mind as we move forward with this section!

DAY 62

I've discovered a six-stage process to facing a fear—ANY fear. It doesn't matter how many fears you face; we all go through the same process over and over again.

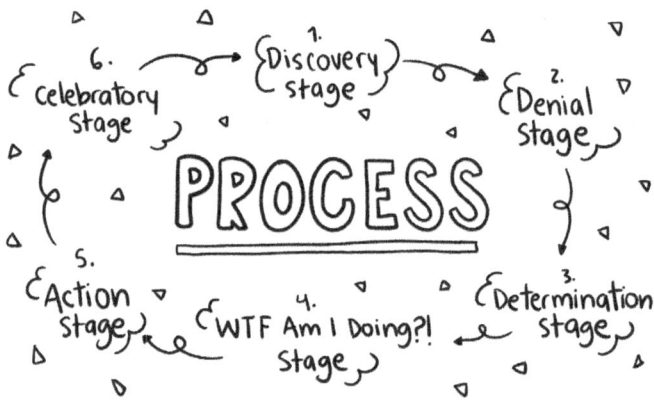

Stage 1, discovery! You've identified and realized something you want to do. Stage 2, immediately after you discover something awesome you want to do, you begin to talk yourself out of it. "I'm not in shape to do that," "I could never afford that," or "That's not something I could do." Stage 3 is when you say "Hey, yes, I can do this! And I WILL!" Then comes stage 4: WTF am I doing?! This is when you ask yourself "What did I get myself into?" Before you actually tackle the fear and take action and certainly before you celebrate your success, this stage is where I want you to exist.

Today, your challenge is to think of a time when you faced a fear and write down your process. When did you realize you were afraid or uncomfortable doing that thing? Did you go into the denial stage without even realizing it? What made you go into the determination stage, and what action steps did you take there? Describe your "WTF am I doing" stage and what helped you overcome it. Write about the action stage next; how was it? How did you celebrate?

DAY 63

Only the very, very brave are able to get beyond their worst thoughts and move past this stage into action, and I have a very simple solution so you can become one of them!

Today, I want you to ask yourself, "What's the BEST that can happen?" if you choose to move forward with the scarier path that you chose on Day 61. Write down five possible rewards that taking action could bring you.

DAY 64

Now that you've moved past the WTF stage, let's talk action! This stage is the moment you shift. It's where you say, "Thanks for everything, but I quit!" or "Hey, Dad, I'm gay!" or "Three, two, one, jump!" or "I do" or "One-way ticket to Thailand, please. Yep, just one!" or "I want a divorce, and I'm keeping the cactus!"

This is the departure from your comfort zone, the moment you take the plunge! If you're here, in your comfort zone, waiting to accomplish your goals, what's your moment of departure? **Choose a date and visualize that moment going better than expected!** Write using past tense to describe how the day went and the positive result from your fear-facing experience.

DAY 65

Afraid to fail? We all are. Tbh, things can go south from time to time, and the best that can happen may not always be what actually happens. But what if the universe is rooting for us? And, even when things don't go according to plan, other wonderful things arise?

Your challenge today is to imagine things don't go as you visualized them yesterday. In fact, imagine you fail. Now answer this question: What's the BEST that can happen if the WORST happens?

That is the question my therapist asked me when I told her about the high expectations I had regarding my book! I answered that question honestly in an essay, but what I never imagined was a pandemic hitting in the middle of my book launch! Even though I was heartbroken at first, thanks to COVID-19, lots of people had the time to actually read my book and feel inspired to overcome bigger obstacles during 2020.

Sometimes, the worst can turn out to be the best.

DAY 66

Have you ever felt proud of yourself ? Like very proud? Like doing a happy dance kind of proud? That's the celebratory stage. I know for a fact that I never felt that kind of proud of myself before in my life until I took my 100-day challenge. I mean, I graduated from college with a 4.0 GPA, I married an amazing man, I got what I thought was my dream job, I did all the things I was expected to do and feel pride in...but those things weren't outside my comfort zone. So accomplishing them didn't make me feel particularly *proud* of myself. I thought: *Check! One less thing I need to worry about.*

But proud? Nah. Proud, real proud, is what you feel when you want something so bad that you're willing to fight the "WTF am I doing?" stage and take action.

Today's challenge is to stop and celebrate those moments of true pride you've experienced in your life. What makes you proud of yourself? If you haven't felt that level of pride before, what do you think it would take to do so?

DAY 67

Growth is personal; what may be growth for me may be comfort for you and vice versa. And what is growth for you today could turn into comfort a few months or years from now. Only you can determine what growth means for you in this moment.

What's magical is that regardless of what growth means for you, when you decide to share that story with others, that simple act of choosing courage can inspire many to do the same. Fear is one of the most relatable feelings in the world; that's why it has so much power. You can infect someone with fear, or you can dose them with courage.

Today's challenge is to share a simple act of courage. Tell your mom or your best friend, or share on social media, about a time you acted courageous. But spread the word and get someone in your network to feel inspired.

How'd it go? Reflect on your action and results in the space provided.

DAY 68

Growth is taking control of our own happiness and our own destinies.

G is being intentional when designing our lives
R is doing everything in our power to achieve our goals
O is ignoring others' opinions and following our hearts
W is being the heroes of our own lives, not the victims
T is freedom
H is a choice

Today, I'd like to challenge you to look at how you define growth and explore it.

What is GROWTH for you?

_____
_____
_____
_____
_____
_____
_____
_____
_____
_____
_____
_____
_____

DAY 69

Growth is almost always the scariest option on the table, which is why it is almost always the path you should choose. When you are pushing boundaries and striving to grow beyond this challenge, it should become easier and easier to choose growth over fear. But in those difficult moments, I want you to keep this in mind: your fear is nothing compared to your bravery.

Since we started sixty-eight days (!) ago, you've come a long way! **What has been the hardest challenge for you so far? And what has been your biggest reward?**

DAY 70

Before moving on to the next section, I am challenging you to commit to growth. To do that, I ask you to sign this contract with yourself:

I, _____, commit to choosing GROWTH over comfort every chance that I get. Because I BELIEVE in myself, I deserve to be happy, and my future is in MY hands.

For my personal journey, this includes:

_____
_____
_____
_____
_____
_____
_____
_____

(your signature here)

EIGHT
hell-(n)o, HECK YES!

> LEARNING HOW TO ASK FOR THE THINGS YOU WANT, NEED, AND DESERVE

In the *Hello, Fears* book, this chapter is about becoming the most assertive person you know.

DAY 71

As Derek Sivers put it, "If you're not saying 'Hell yeah!' about something, say no." As we touched on last week, setting boundaries and saying no is the only way to say yes to what you actually want. For some reason, we think it is okay to put ourselves, our needs, and our wants last. It is NOT okay!

Today, I am challenging you to take a look at your to-do list. Not just the goals you have shared at other points in this journey but your *actual* to-do list for this week. I want you to circle everything that is for YOU and do all those things FIRST.

*Note, if you don't have anything on your to-do list for yourself, time to add some things ASAP!

DAY 72

Allow me to introduce you to the concept of the polite decline! Saying no doesn't have to mean "I don't care about you" or "I don't like you!" It just means "I have other priorities right now" or "I need to do this for myself." Taking action for yourself means declining some actions for others.

Today, I'd like to challenge you to think of something you did recently that you really should have declined taking onto your plate. Use the space below to write out what it was and what you wish you had said to get out of it! Use this as a script for next time.

DAY 72

DAY 73

One of the hardest things to keep in mind when taking action is actually *setting boundaries*. Before you say yes to something, you always need to ask yourself: *Am I saying yes because I don't want to disappoint other people or because I'm genuinely excited to commit and it will help me move forward in my goals?*

I made a list of the things that matter most to me right now (promoting my book, being with my baby, spending quality time with Adam, recording my own podcast, spending time with friends and family), so every time I get a new request, I check my list, and if it doesn't align with my priorities, then it becomes a clear "no thanks!"

Today's challenge is to write up your list of yeses so that moving forward, you know when to clearly say NO!

DAY 74

As you begin to assert your goals for yourself with others, it can be easy to approach things from a perspective of aggression or force. However, the best way to get things done is to fight with kindness and to trust your values as a way to stand up for yourself. It can be easy to lose ourselves in our race to our goals and everything we have on our agendas, but you can gain support for your goals if you simply explain your priorities with kindness and empathy.

One of my favorite hacks to confront someone and establish clear boundaries is to write what I want to say first. **I challenge you to identify something you are expected to do by someone else, something you realized will take away time from what you actually want to do.** Now, write the script of what you'd like to tell that person. Take your time and revise it with someone you trust. I know you don't want to disappoint others, but you will feel so relieved once you don't have that weight on your shoulders. Do it for your future self!

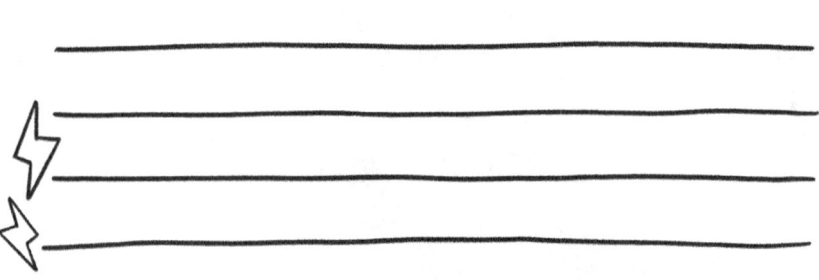

DAY 75

One of the biggest reasons to become more assertive is to start making decisions NOW versus putting things off from a place of fear or discomfort. In fact, we go to great lengths to avoid discomfort. It is one of the fear categories we are all most keen to avoid! But you need to consider what you want to do now versus what you want to do most. Too often, we choose NOW without realizing we are screwing our future selves up!

Today, I challenge you to identify what you want now and what you want most. See if there is some overlap that we can begin to tackle this week!

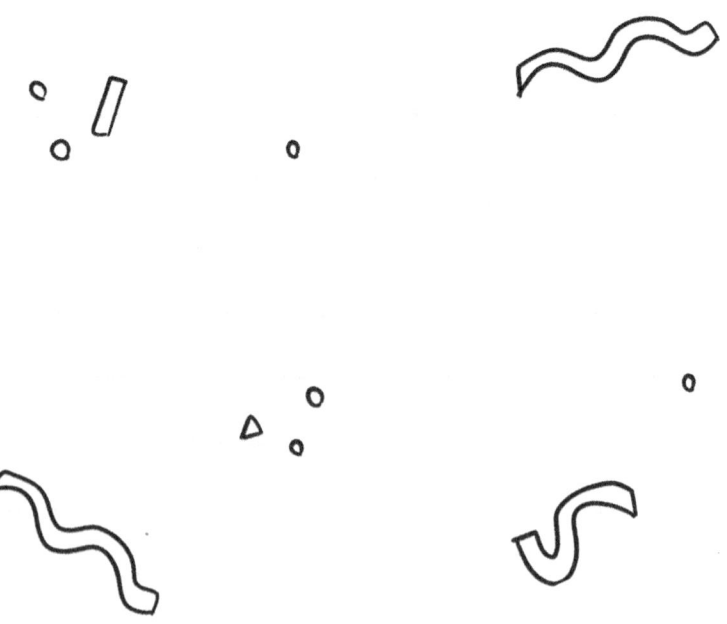

I can attack the overlap by...
_____
_____
_____

DAY 76

Taking last week's discomfort avoidance in stride, it's time to get rejected! Rejection is something we all try to avoid, but by avoiding the fear of rejection, we are avoiding taking chances on ourselves!

As my rejection-savvy friend Jia Jiang shared in the interview featured in our book, "When you decide not to try, you are not competing against rejection; you are simply rejecting yourself."

Today's challenge is for you to put yourself out there in as many ways as you can with the goal of getting rejected. When we aim for rejection, we ask for what we want in a more unapologetic way, more authentically, and with less fear. Looking for approval is so hard that we say what we think others want to hear instead of what we actually want to say. Dare to ask for as many things as you can today. If you don't get rejected, it doesn't count! Haha.

Examples: Ask your partner for a massage. Ask your boss for a promotion. Ask your coworker for a recommendation on LinkedIn. Ask an influencer for a LIVE on Instagram. And so on!

These are the things I will attempt today as a way to seek (rejection)

_____
_____
_____
_____
_____
_____
_____
_____
_____
_____

Unapologetically,

_____
(your name)

DAY 77

One of the things people struggle the most with is asking for HELP. We feel as if we should have everything figured out, and the truth is that if we want to go fast, we have to go on our own, but if we want to go FAR, we have to go together. I love to help others but also to ask for help. This has been KEY in my personal growth.

Today, I am challenging you to identify the areas in which you could use help as a way to go further. Maybe you need better designs, better copy, someone to help out with your baby or the house. Maybe you need help to become more assertive, a better presenter, or a more confident leader. It's okay to ask for help! Perhaps that person who you need also needs something from you. When you get vulnerable and ask for help, others will do the same with you!

DAY 78

As we move forward in our journey of action and assertion, one of my biggest obstacles was the idea of perfection. I eventually had a breakthrough moment when I stopped overthinking (and wasting time!) and decided to choose action over perfection.

Today, I challenge you to let go of an ideal that is holding you back from taking action. It could be perfection, as was my case. It could be feeling undeserving until you hit a certain milestone, or like you're certain to fail unless you have things perfectly timed. However, when we decide to choose momentum over perfection, amazing things can happen—expected and otherwise. What do you need to let go of in order to thrive?

DAY 79

In my transition from a place of inaction to action, I realized one of the biggest lies I continued to tell myself was that I had more time. I didn't need to push for my goals right this minute, not when there was all the time in the world! Unfortunately, this was both a false sense of security (none of us knows how much time we have) as well as yet another way I was keeping myself complacent in my goals. While theoretically "there's always tomorrow," if you always wait for tomorrow, you'll never experience your goals today!

Your challenge is to look at your big dreams, the ones you've been putting off and holding close to your heart but telling yourself you'll tackle tomorrow/next year/before XYZ. Which can one you start going after TODAY?

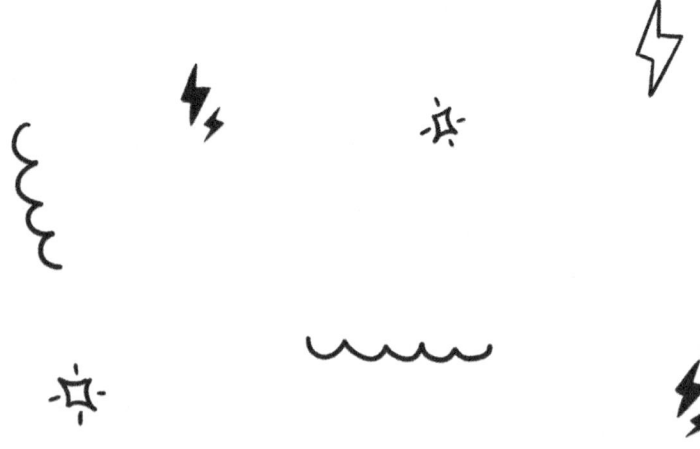

DAY 80

The final hurdle to becoming assertive is when you are plagued by indecision. How can you move forward if you aren't sure which way you want to go?

When faced with two choices, both of which are theoretically promising, I've found that the best tool to making a decision is to listen to my instincts. Take time to process your options and really listen to how you are physically and mentally reacting to each. Look at why you are tempted to say yes to something: Are your reasons all your own? Are they all coming from a place of bravery versus fear?

Today, your challenge is to explore a decision currently on your plate that you find yourself struggling with. List the pros and cons for each, noting WHY you would decide to move forward with each option, and see if that doesn't bring you closer to a resolution!

OPTION 1

PROS	CONS

OPTION 2

PROS	CONS

NINE
hello, SUCCESS

HOW NOT TO SELF-SABOTAGE YOUR WAY TO SUCCESS

In the Hello, Fears book, this chapter is about making it really big.

DAY 81

If you have made it this far in the challenge, you are CLEARLY a finisher! This section is all about the last fear to explore before we reach the final challenges: *fear of success.*

But before we dive into what a fear of success may look like, we first have to define success. **So today, your challenge is to take a moment and write out your own definition of success, according to what you value, and then draw a few elements that represent success to you.** This is very personal, so leave aside the typical definition for success and focus only on the things that bring you genuine happiness.

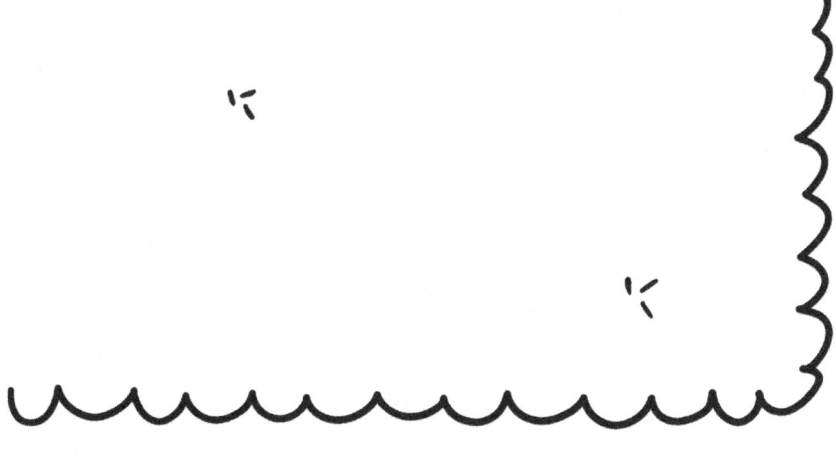

DAY 82

Now that you've defined what success is to you, let's discuss what success is NOT! Success to me involves travel, speaking, and making an impact. For others, it is a quiet life at home with creature comforts.

Today, your challenge is to outline what success ISN'T to you, though it may be the definition of success to others! The last thing you want is to become successful at something you don't enjoy or that isn't in your end goals, so this list will become your list to avoid!

DAY 82

DAY 83

One of the trickiest aspects of success is that, as outlined by what success is and isn't to you, sometimes we are super successful and skilled at things that we don't care one iota about!

Skills are the things we are naturally good at. The more we work on them, the better we get. Passions are the things that bring us fulfillment or joy when we practice them. We don't necessarily need to be good at them, but they bring us joy!

Today's challenge is to look at your skills and your passions. Circle where there are overlaps that you can monopolize on and grow your success!

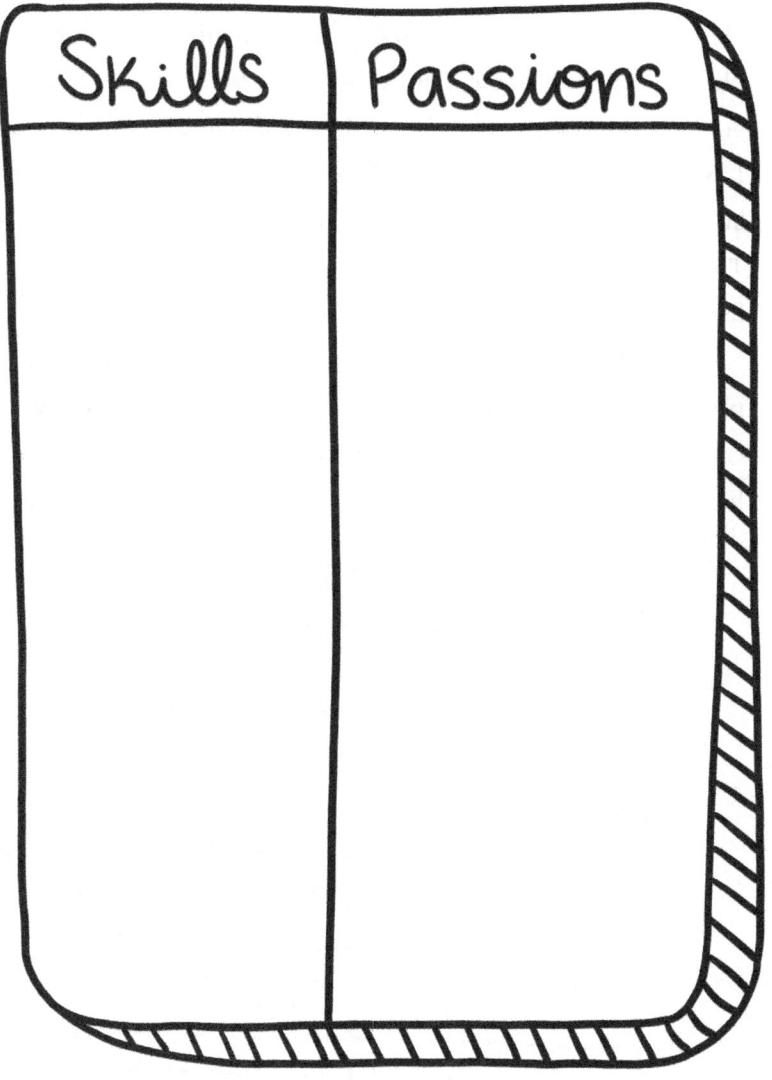

DAY 84

Now that you have your vision for success in mind, we can grapple with the first component of a fear of success: losing what you have now to gain the life you dream of living. For Adam and I, when we moved to New York to pursue our dreams, we left behind a beautiful life we had established for ourselves in Miami. There was nothing wrong with our lifestyle—in fact, it could have been a dream come true for many! It simply wasn't for us.

Today, your challenge is to explore what you'll sacrifice by following your biggest dreams. Make sure each is acknowledged and recognized so you can comfortably let them go and look forward! Here are some of mine. What do yours look like?

What I Sacrifice	What I Get
Weekends	Being my own boss
Living near family & friends	Living in NYC, our favorite place on Earth
Owning a car and a house	Total freedom to move around as we please
Babies	Fully focusing on our career for now
9-5 Job stability	The opportunity to grow exponentially
Leisure time	Getting good stuff done
Routine	New experiences

What I Sacrifice	What I Get

DAY 85

For today's challenge, I am replicating an exercise from my book, Hello, Fears! If you've already done this in the book pages, try it again now with a new goal! If you skipped it last time to keep reading (I know how compelling it can be!), now's your chance to participate and grow!

Imagine you set a pretty high goal for yourself for next year, one that has the potential to change your life. What would that goal be? Dare to dream big for this exercise. Maybe it's reaching one hundred thousand followers, launching a successful product or store, getting published, going on live TV, getting hired by the company of your dreams for the position and the salary of your dreams, or being best friends with your idol. What is that goal?

My GOAL for NEXT YEAR is to:

_____

_____

Now, fast-forward and imagine that you worked tirelessly to make it happen...and you did! Not only did it happen, but it went better than expected! YASSSS! Savor that success for a brief moment. **Now double the size of your dream:**

_____

_____

How do you feel?

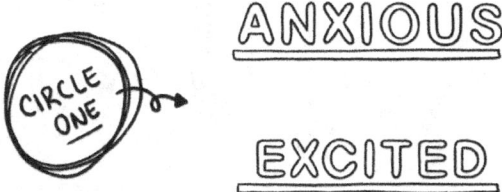

Take a couple of minutes now to write down the positive and the not-so-positive ways in which your life will change now that you've achieved your goal.

Do you still want to achieve your goal?

If you answered "umm, nope," then you need to rethink your goal and do this exercise again until you get "HECK YES!" If you are already there, congratulations! You're ready to move from dreaming to achieving.

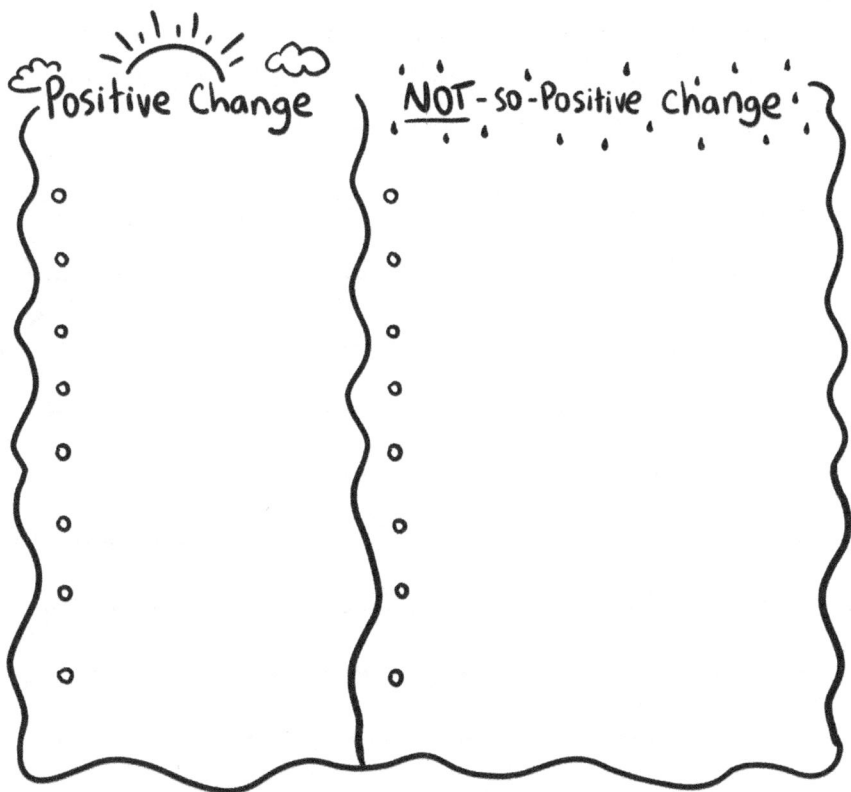

DAY 86

In finding my own version of success, I became a new version of myself.

Just like giving up the perks of our current life for the promise of our new life, by generating your success, you'll become a new version of yourself. **Today, your challenge is to look at the old you, before you started this challenge, and compare them to the new you!** How have you changed in this journey? What does that growth look like?

DAY 87

Once we are nearing success, our brains can get triggered and try to trip us into failure with self-sabotage. When this happens, we embody one of these three personas, or all of them at the same time:

Persona #1: The Impostor. You convince yourself that you are no expert on this subject, so you must do some *more* research before you actually publish that blog post about this thing you are so passionate about.

Persona #2: The Undervalued. You convince yourself that your content or your product is only *somewhat* valuable, and you will feel better about yourself if you would just give it away for *free*.

Persona #3: The Perfectionist. You convince yourself that it is almost ready, but not there yet. So you delay your launch date again and again, because there is *always* something you can review one more time and improve.

Sound familiar? Today's challenge is to get over these limiting beliefs that are tripping you up right as you are on the cusp of success! Simply move forward, hit upload, submit your work for that award, launch, or whatever it is that you have been waiting to do! Use the space on the next page to outline what you put forward and how you feel!

DAY 88

Remember the big goal that I asked you to envision a few pages ago? The one that was double your goal for this year? Now imagine one more time that it materialized. You worked hard AF, and you made it happen! You celebrate, you savor your well-deserved success, and...now what?

There is nothing more terrifying to me than a fulfilled dream, because it only means one thing: you now need to come up with a new dream. Turns out, life keeps going, and it is our job to continue reinventing ourselves. Better to do so than to end up in our comfort zones.

Today's challenge is to come up with five new goals to chase once your BIG goal is off your list. Assume in your brainstorming that you've accomplished your first, BIG dream and these are your next steps!

1. _____
2. _____
3. _____
4. _____
5. _____

{ NEW GOALS! }

DAY 89

As you look to grow and build on your success with bigger, broader goals, you need to keep the guilt of success at bay. Success can be pretty lonely if you ride that wave solo. You will go from having a similar life to that of the people around you to suddenly having the awesome life you envisioned. And the truth is that you will have opportunities that no one else in your circle will, and that can bring guilt to many, which can prevent you from enjoying the success you accomplished through hard work.

As Brené Brown says, the only way to fight the terrifying emotion of joy is not by feeling guilt but by practicing gratitude. The people who experience joy are not the most successful, the most accomplished, or the most loved. They are the people who practice gratitude.

Today, success or no, your challenge is to stop and be thankful. What are the good things happening in your life, right now, that you will always be thankful for and appreciate?

DAY 89

DAY 90

As a final note on success, as a society, we are often told to diminish our success to help others feel bigger. This is, to be frank, bullshit. TAKE UP SPACE WITH YOUR SUCCESS. We are often told we take up too much space, that we are too loud, too quiet, too emotional, too smart, too dramatic. FORGET THAT!

Today's challenge is for you to take up space and NOT apologize for it. This unapologetic space-taking, in itself, is a revolutionary act. You are BANNED from saying "I'm sorry" today (and ideally moving forward!). Find other modes of communication, but do not apologize for your goals. The moment you find yourself wanting to apologize, come back here and explain yourself to your journal. You got this!

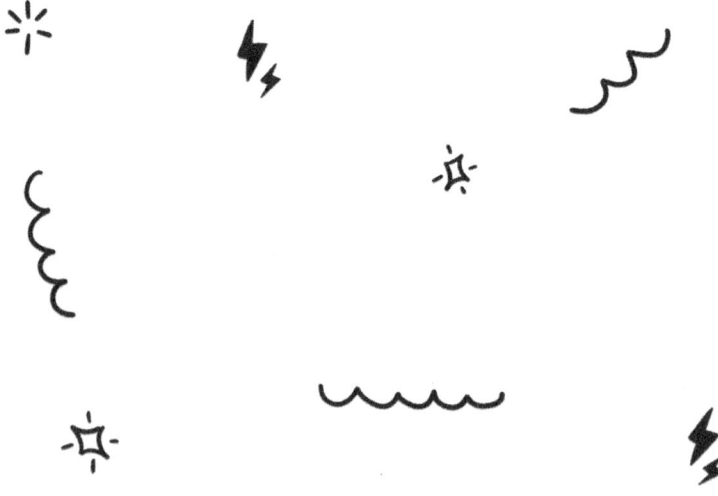

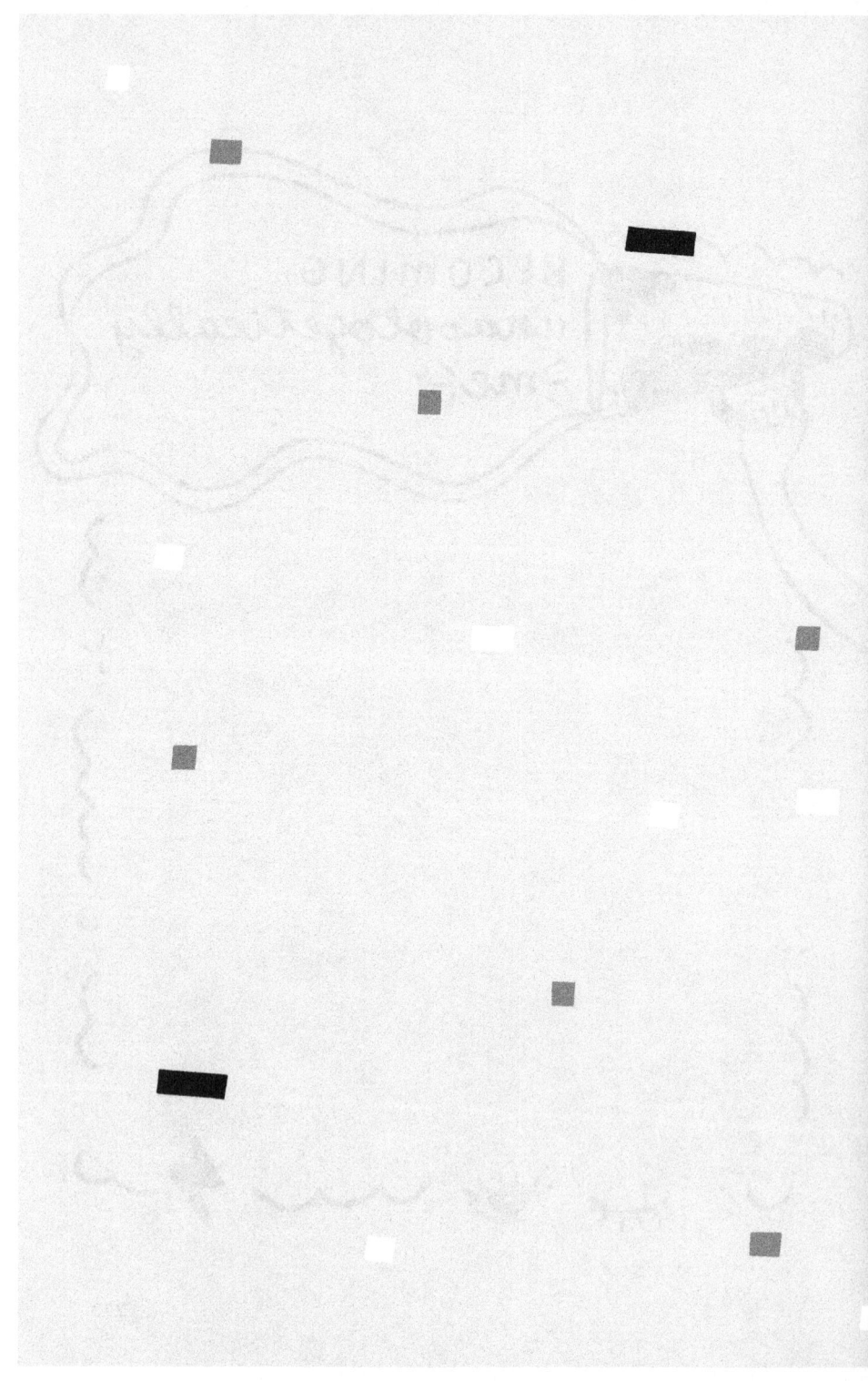

TEN

hello, FUTURE

> ## GROW THROUGH DIRT—REWRITE YOUR STORY

In the Hello, Fears book, this chapter is about using our pasts to uncover our purpose.

DAY 91

We're in the FINAL COUNTDOWN of the challenge! OMG, look at how far you've come! You're such a BRAVE BADASS! As we enter the final phase of the challenge, we are looking at everything that has shaped us into who we are and what we will take with us in our journey forward.

So to that end, let's take a moment to look at who you were BEFORE you started this journey. **Today's challenge is to get honest and vulnerable about who you were and now where you are going.** What's changed in these first ninety days? What are you still scared of? What are you excited about?

DAY 92

Being independent was never a goal of mine. I could spend hours with someone I didn't like as long as I didn't have to go somewhere by myself. Have you ever done that? Honestly, I loved having my parents do everything for me growing up and then my friends and Adam as a young adult. I used to think of myself as too fragile and unreliable. And I kind of liked having people look after me. It made me feel protected at all times.

Independence can be scary, but it doesn't HAVE to be. In fact, it can be a blessing. **Today, your challenge is to look at where your dependencies lie.** What are some things you should break free of so you can stand on your own? What are some that you should lean into for support as you move forward in your goals?

DAY 92

DAY 93

As Frida Kahlo said, "Échame tierra y verás como florezco." ("Throw dirt at me and watch me bloom.") Your struggles are what make you who are you are today, feeding you and helping you grow. Taking the example of flowers growing from dirt, can you identify your dirt?

Dirt can obviously be messy, gritty, and hard to find potential in, but flowers still find the space to grow. Your dirt is a challenge you have, one that makes you believe you have some sort of disadvantage. Maybe it's lack of support, money, or time. Maybe it's a tumultuous past, an abusive relationship, the country you live in, or your family's history.

Today, I challenge you to identify your dirt and write about it. How does it affect your present?

Throw *dirt* at ME and watch **bloom**

DAY 94

We need to believe it is possible to grow from dirt instead of living our entire life stuck in it. Do you see it? For a few moments, try to envision the person you'd like to become mentally, emotionally, and physically. Every reality starts with a vision. I knew I wanted to become a braver person, an example for others, and a thought leader, but I was none of those things just a few years ago.

Today's challenge is to fully focus on the version of yourself you want to become. Blooming is entirely up to us; only we can water ourselves and grow from our dirt. So who do you want to be?

> I want to become
> _____
> _____
> _____
> _____

DAY 95

How can you use your experience to make an impact? In my case, I wanted to become a speaker and share my message so more people could change their perception of fear. One of my goals was to speak to the younger generation and tell them all the things I wish someone had told me when I was their age. Maybe you want to teach something no one taught you or become the boss you never had or create a documentary you wish existed or a book that would've helped you years ago.

Today's challenge is to explore that simple question. If you could do something for your younger self, what would you do?

DAY 96

When we are purpose driven, we ultimately forget about our fears and focus on our actions. This is what turns a thought leader into an action leader. We burst through our own insecurities because we have a purpose to fulfill. Speaking on stage (or virtually) in front of thousands could be terrifying, but what if my message could potentially change the lives of many? How can I say no to that?

Today's challenge is to act out of pure purpose. This means choose someone you want to impact today, and do something positive for that person. Go light someone else's candle! Think about the people who surround you—who needs you the most? How can you go out of your way today to be there for that person?

"a candle loses nothing by lighting another candle"

DAY 97

You're nearing the end of your challenge and moving forward in your goals. Let's take a moment to take stock of where you are and where you want to go. I recently came upon four lists that I had made for myself last year.

1. A list of the things I regretted doing that year or felt sorry for (in terms of my behavior)
2. A list of the things I was grateful for (that was the longest one)
3. A list of the things I asked for (wishes, goals, dreams, and desires)
4. A list of the things I promised myself (a.k.a. my commitment to becoming my best version of myself)

Today, it's your turn. Make your own version of these four lists. What do they show you about your goals and the person you want to become?

DAY 98

As you finish this challenge, you're finishing your transformation from timid to #girlboss. You're becoming a freaking ROCK STAR! For a long time, I thought I was not really a humble person, because I can talk about myself with lots of confidence. I now know my worth and have no problem letting other people know what I've done and what I'm made of.

Most of us believe that to be humble is to hide our own accomplishments to make others feel comfortable. But can't we be humble and NOT downplay our worth?

I believe we can! I redefined being humble as:

- *wanting to share our knowledge, our opportunities, and our tools so more people can rise*
- *being grateful for what we have instead hiding it*
- *sharing our failures as much as our successes to make others feel good about themselves but inspired at the same time*
- *appreciating compliments, understanding we are not perfect, but being okay with praise—we deserve it!*
- *praising others and giving them credit*
- *listening to other people's concerns and ideas*
- *giving selflessly*

Today's challenge is to be humble! As you continue to grow and become an inspiration to your community, how else can you be humble without having to downplay your worth?

DAY 99

They say you can't pour from an empty cup, but what does that mean?

Essentially? It means that you need to TAKE CARE OF YOU! How are you caring for yourself and making sure you aren't running on empty?

You're almost at the finish line of this challenge, and I know I haven't made it easy for you! Almost all these challenges were created to push you further mentally than would normally be comfortable. Heck, in many, discomfort was the specific goal!

Your challenge today is to make sure that even as this challenge ends, you are taking care of yourself and preparing for the next challenge you'll face. Acknowledging that it is okay to take a break, how can you refill yourself this week and make sure that even after this challenge finishes (one more day!), you are taking care to mentally refuel? Remember, going back to the imagery from Frida Kahlo's quote, only you can water yourself. How will you water yourself this week?

DAY 100 (!!!)

One hundred days! YOU DID IT! OMG, YOU ARE SUCH A BRAVE BADASS! Congratulations on accomplishing this amazing feat of facing and tackling your fears!

I've got wonderful news for you: just because this challenge has ended doesn't mean you're done with your journey! In fact, you're very likely just starting out on the real adventure!

A few days ago, I asked you to write your story, remember? I now want you to write what comes next. Imagine you are twenty years from today! What are some of the things you accomplished? DREAM BIG...BIGGER!

P.S. When you catch yourself comparing your journey to the journey of someone you already admire, remember the years and the hard work that person had to go through to get where they are. You'll get there too. Remember: "Never compare your beginning to someone else's middle."

SOMETIMES the things we want THE MOST are just ONE act of COURAGE away

- Putting myself out there
- Starting your own Business
- Feeling all EMOTIONS
- Saying NO! to others
- Living the life you decide
- Letting GO
- Writing a Book
- Trying new things
- Leaving your partner
- Leaving a job you don't like
- Opening up
- Saying YES to myself
- Moving to a new country
- Taking the next step

100 CHALLENGES LATER

You Did It!

HOW DO YOU FEEL?!

Just as I ended the *Hello, Fears* book, I'd like to end this journal with a reflection and an exercise. I encourage you to write a short letter to your future self. Write the current date and the date you want to open this letter in the future. Make a commitment to yourself. Let your future self know that you will work hard now to make them proud later. And then, fold the page in half and use a sticker to close it. Put a reminder on your phone for the day you wish to open this letter so you won't forget. This could be a one-year commitment, a three-year commitment, or even a ten-year commitment—you choose!

Putting things in writing has enormous power. It gives us clarity on our goals and the confidence that we can make them happen. It also helps put our ideas into the universe and serves as a promise that we make to ourselves. What can be more sacred than that?

Optional: Attach a picture of your current self to this section and use this as a time capsule. Now go out there and put everything you learned into action so you too can pursue your passion, make choices that work for YOU, become your most authentic self, and go confidently after your dream, so when that moment comes for you to open this chapter again, you'll say, "Michelle, you were so right." Because you know what? You deserve to live your best life.

Sometimes the things we want the most are just one act of courage away.

Dear future self,
_____
_____
_____
_____
_____
_____
_____

ABOUT THE AUTHOR

BORN AND RAISED IN CARACAS, Venezuela, Michelle Poler is a creative and passionate fear facer, keynote speaker, social entrepreneur, and branding strategist.

Michelle was accustomed to living with fear, but when she moved to New York to pursue a master's degree in branding at the School of Visual Arts, she quickly realized that the Big Apple was not for the fearful. To change her approach to life, Michelle decided to face 100 of her fears in a period of 100 days, uploading every experience to YouTube, where the project quickly became a viral phenomenon.

Facing her fears took Michelle to a TEDx stage, and this decision marked the beginning of her speaking career. Since then, she has given talks at companies such as Google, Facebook, LinkedIn, Netflix, Microsoft, P&G, Toyota, Coca-Cola, Yum! Brands, Wells Fargo, and many more, as well as inspired more than 100,000 students from all over the world at schools and leadership organizations.

Michelle and her husband, Adam, used to travel about 120 times per year, and as they did, they started a Spanish-language podcast, Desde El Avión (From the Plane), as they flew from event to event. Now that they have become parents, they added a new cohost to their show, baby Noah, and are recording most of their episodes from the nursery!

Michelle also teaches people how to become "unapologetically them" through her online programs and manages her Hello Fears community on Instagram (@hellofears) and Patreon, empowering thousands to step outside their comfort zones and tap into their full potential every day.

Made in United States
North Haven, CT
03 September 2024